Plain talk to young executives

Plain talk to
young executives

PAUL M. HAMMAKER
and
LOUIS T. RADER

1977

RICHARD D. IRWIN, INC. *Homewood, Illinois 60430*
IRWIN-DORSEY LIMITED *Georgetown, Ontario L7G 4B3*

First Printing, April 1977

ISBN 0-87094-137-2
Library of Congress Catalog Card No. 76-49317
Printed in the United States of America

This book is dedicated to
the Rader families
and to
Bishop and Mrs. Wilbur E. Hammaker,
their sons and wives,
their grandsons and wives, and
their great grandchildren.

Preface

The purpose of this book is to guide young men and women who want to become leaders in organizations, that is, to become managers.

The problems of managers in the early part of their careers are very real. Often they want help and have very little to guide them. To a considerable extent some men and women who have advanced into middle management also feel the need for guidance.

We have made certain assumptions about you, the readers of this book:

1. You have decided you want to be a good manager.
2. You are now a manager or expect to be one soon.
3. You strongly desire to be successful and will put forth the necessary effort to learn, decide, and act in order to achieve success.
4. You wish to achieve a managerial position that will allow you to utilize all your capabilities, talents, and skill. This often means working for and securing a promotion to a higher level managing position.
5. You want to achieve happiness which results in part from work well done, adequately recognized, and well compensated.

We have tried to draw on our own common sense, experiences, and education to develop those principles that we feel are fundamental to successful management. We emphasize that the readers must establish their own frames of reference and their own benchmarks, and should not take what we say as the only possible solution. Various techniques and ideas from real life presented in this book offer readers the opportunity to adopt a technique that may meet their needs or to select for their own use an idea that has been successful for others. In the appendix to this book we have also provided our answers to the questions young managers most frequently ask us.

We think it is better to light one candle than to curse the darkness. We think this book might serve individual young managers as a candle. If they can embrace and implement a goodly number of the ideas in this book, the illumination will magnify.

As you begin your reading, the authors wish you Bon Voyage!

March 1977   PAUL M. HAMMAKER
                               LOUIS T. RADER

Authors' note 1:
On Him/Her

At times when referring to managers, we say such things as:

"if he/she wants to be successful . . ."

"he/she has little choice other than having a positive attitude . . ."

"to clarify his/her thinking . . ."

Where many places we use *he* and *him*, these pronouns are meant by the authors to include both sexes.

One of the authors has been responsible directly and indirectly for managing from half a dozen to over 300 women managers. He has found them to encompass about the same percentage of very superior, well-above average, and average managers as similar groups of men.

Not only do the authors lack bias on the male/female manager question, but they predict a steadily increasing percentage of managers will be women.

P. M. H.
L. T. R.

Authors' note 2:
On managing in
nonprofit institutions

As managers of nonprofit institutions will clearly see, the authors have addressed themselves to managers of private enterprises that must earn a profit if they are to survive over time.

Many great American institutions including universities, hospitals, foundations, and government live and operate in a different realm. They are supported by endowments or are tax supported.

Despite the fact that the authors address those in profit-making concerns, the first six principles covered as well as many other portions of this book, have applicability to nonprofit institution managers.

Managers in nonprofit institutions are specifically addressed in Chapter 10.

P. M. H.
L. T. R.

Contents

I think having sound beliefs and having them clearly in mind is an essential first factor for achieving more than ordinary success in managing.

I believe every person is an individual and is unique and is a man or woman of dignity, merit, and worth.

I think your attitudes flow out of your beliefs. I believe that attitudes affect significantly your managing style. It affects significantly the results you achieve. Your results are one vital measurement of your success.

If your present beliefs, attitudes and behavior patterns are not what you want them to be, you aren't stuck with them. You can improve them if you wish to and will do the necessary work.

Paul M. Hammaker

I believe it is as necessary for mental health to have convictions and beliefs as it is for physical health to have nutrition and exercise. Otherwise, the modern would will be as grim as Yeats stated:

"The best lack all conviction, the worst are full of passionate intensity."

Louis T. Rader

1

Some basic convictions and beliefs about life and managing

The four most important things characteristic of many young managers are:

1. The desire to live a fully satisfying life.
2. The desire to achieve their full potential in all areas of life, be it business, social, family, or others.
3. The desire to manage successfully, since this contributes to the achievement of objectives one and two.
4. The desire to become a successful, mature, established manager.

There is no value in discussing such important matters as management functions, management techniques, management style, motivation techniques, and leadership—before we have addressed ourselves to the most fundamental fact about each individual manager. That fact is the set of convictions and beliefs that every individual young manager has developed. Some young managers' convictions and beliefs are clearer, more comprehensive, and better coordinated than others—but *all* do have their own individual set of them.

These convictions and beliefs color their personalities, are the source of their attitudes, set their managing style, determine how people will react to them, and influence the degree of success they will achieve.

The authors have observed hundreds of managers and discovered that the ones achieving the most success have clear and sound basic convictions and beliefs. Among young managers these convictions tend to be constant and change little in their early years as managers. Later, as they become more mature and carefully examine changes taking place in the total social, economic, and political environment, as well as in their personal lives, they usually rethink their convictions and beliefs—with the result that some new ones are added and some old ones are given different weight, while some early convictions are modified or dropped.

In a very few cases that we have observed, managers have drastically changed their convictions and beliefs. A nonbusiness example of very great change is that of the biblical character Saul of Tarsus, who saw the light and as a result adopted beliefs —as Paul—that were 100 percent different from those he had held. This type of revolutionary change is experienced by few managers, but though drastic changes in convictions do not usually occur, successful managers change in many other ways over the years, particularly in relation to improving their technical managing skills, their techniques of planning, leading, and directing people, helping people develop their full potential, controlling, measuring, rewarding excellence, and punishing failure.

Because this book is designed to help young managers and not just tell them, we now introduce a question which we hope you, the reader, will answer to yourself: Do you believe it is advantageous for a manager to know clearly what his convictions are? If so, you and the authors are together. If not, it would be interesting to jot down why clarity of your personal convictions is not important to your success in managing.

As an idea starter, here is another query: What is the source of your attitudes? Are they your basic beliefs, such as people are lazy, leading to an attitude—you can't depend on them to do the necessary work on time and in a first-class manner—leading to you bossing people in a stern, authoritarian manner, or are your beliefs on people almost the exact opposite?

The authors are convinced that having sound beliefs and knowing clearly and comprehensively what they are is an essential first factor in achieving more than ordinary success in managing.

An illustration of some basic convictions is furnished by John D. Rockefeller, Jr.'s beliefs:

I believe

I believe in the supreme worth of the individual and in his right to life, liberty, and the pursuit of happiness.

I believe that every right implies a responsibility; every opportunity, an obligation; every possession, a duty.

I believe that the law was made for man and not man for the law; that government is the servant of the people and not their master.

I believe in the dignity of labor, whether with head or hand; that the world owes no man a living but that it owes every man an opportunity to make a living.

I believe that thrift is essential to well-ordered living and that economy is a prime requisite of a sound financial structure, whether in government, business or personal affairs.

I believe that truth and justice are fundamental to an enduring social order.

I believe in the sacredness of a promise, that a man's word should be as good as his bond; that character— not wealth or power or position—is of supreme worth.

I believe that the rendering of useful service is the common duty of mankind and that only in the purifying fire of sacrifice is the dross of selfishness consumed and the greatness of the human soul set free.

I believe in an all-wise and all-loving God, named by whatever name, and that the individual's highest fulfillment, greatest happiness, and widest usefulness are to be found in living in harmony with His will.

I believe that love is the greatest thing in the world; that it alone can overcome hate; that right can and will triumph over might.

John D. Rockefeller, Jr.

As a young manager, what do you find in the Rockefeller credo that seems to you to be questionable or, in fact, from your point of view, inapplicable, if not clearly wrong?

Please look more deeply at Rockefeller's ideas, because your success as a manager depends upon the skill with which you sort out ideas and latch on to the ones you consider good and reject the ones that you consider irrelevant or bad. And since a great deal of your business life is going to consist of absorbing information, reaching conclusions, and making decisions, it is quite appropriate that you should settle now on the Rockefeller beliefs that you think are useful and helpful to you. Do you get a single idea which you consider to have merit from your study of the Rockefeller credo? If you do, it certainly should not be adopted and be part of your belief at this particular moment, because usually instant answers are not good. Take your time, digest the thought and its implications. Does the new idea square with your other ideas?

We believe that mental health and self-confidence and the ability to manage well are dependent on knowing what your beliefs are so that you do not get whipsawed every time you get into economic or some other type of discussion. The ultimate result of being whipsawed frequently or being a helpless chip on a turbulent stream who responds instantly to whatever is at hand not only makes for poor mental health but is almost a guarantee that you will not be a great success as a manager.

Following is a portion of the beliefs of the authors.

1. We are all children of God.
2. In this particular way we are equal.
3. As children of God we are brothers. This is the basic idea behind the brotherhood of man.

4. Our brotherhood though not fully realized is a basis for:

   Getting along with people.
   A community of interest.
   Voluntary cooperative effort.
   Hope of peace in the world.

5. Every man and woman are individuals of dignity, merit and worth because they are children of God.
6. Every individual is different and unique and precious in the sight of God.
7. We believe in the search for truth, beauty and greatness.
8. Our goal is to achieve the one covered in a few words from a much repeated prayer, namely, "Thy will be done."
9. Who will do His will? We can. You can.
10. Is it hard to do His will? Yes. We start as selfish animals crying for food and demanding attention; everything is getting and there is no giving.

    We know that primitive people are quite selfish and can be very savage.

    We know that uncivilized people are not overly careful of the rights and safety of people outside the family or tribe. All others are their enemy. This is a far cry from the theory of the brotherhood of man.
11. What can create a situation where each individual is regarded as a person of dignity, merit and worth and where he can have acknowledged rights and safety?

    One such thing that can bring about this condition is acceptance of religious beliefs and ideas. We believe that if we walk humbly, act justly, worship God and make an honorable living that we have contributed something of value to our family, neighbors, and country.
12. Legitimate business is an honorable activity. Business is in bad odor with many Americans today. We believe that U.S. business is basically good and beneficial to the country and, therefore, take the opportunity to comment on it favorably, to explain it, and to recommend it as opportunities exist.

    If U.S. citizens truly desire to and do in fact minimize business, through increased regulations, giving overriding priorities to ecological and other aspects which allegedly would make for a higher quality of living, then the country will have a declining standard of living and a poorer place in international competition. However, we believe in the wisdom of the U.S. people and should they elect these things, we would accept their decision.

13. We are not helpless chips on a turbulent stream but are largely masters of our destiny.

14. There are enduring values and basic truths. Some that we believe in are:

The existence of God.

Self-centeredness equals personal dissatisfaction.

Giving is not only more blessed, it is more satisfying to the individual than getting.

Those who live by the sword, die by it.

The hope of mankind is enlightened self-interest and practice of the idea of the brotherhood of man.

We see some differences between the Rockefeller credo and the portion of our beliefs just covered. For example, the Rockefeller credo is more comprehensive. However, our interest is not in Rockefeller's beliefs and ours, but in yours. Are there things in the authors' beliefs that you think are plainly wrong or useless or invalid? If so, identify them and thus help clarify your own thoughts and reinforce your own values.

Because we believe in emphasizing the positive, and because often the greater rewards go to the enthusiast, we ask now that you turn your attention to what there is in our beliefs that can be useful to you. What is there that you can embrace enthusiastically? Now pause! If you are about to embrace a new view that is somewhat unknown or deals with an area you haven't thought about much, we caution against instant decisions and an instant change of conviction.

As an aside, it is interesting to contemplate that as the speed of communication increases there appears to be among businessmen a feeling that decisions need to be made equally rapidly. We believe that now, more than in the past, senior executives think they have to decide an issue immediately. As you will see, this is at odds with one of our thoughts. We believe most major issues do not have to be decided immediately. However, many of the operating decisions made by young managers do need to be made immediately. They normally do not deal with matters of basic principles but instead with something of a rather normal or routine nature that is within the parameters of prescribed company objectives, policies, and procedures.

A former GE vice president, Lem Boulware, used to preach that businessmen should "Do what is right voluntarily." A lot of people believe this shows a naïve approach to labor relations or human relations but we believe if you have clarified what is right, you can do and should do it voluntarily in most areas of business before pressures are applied. If, on the other hand, you have no strong feelings as to what is right or wrong morally, ethically, economically, then, of course, your decision making becomes very difficult and you have an equal chance of making bad decisions as good ones. Managers whose batting average is only 50 percent become ex-managers. We believe you should be "right" at least 80 percent of the time.

Perhaps you are surprised at the use of the words *right* and *wrong* in the previous paragraph. In the 20th century the idea has grown that some things are right—white, and some things are wrong—black, but most things fall in the grey area. That is either a polite way of saying there are a lot of things neither right nor wrong or that we are unable to determine on a given issue whether it is right or wrong so we put it in the grey area. However, a manager facing a specific issue has to make the decision sooner or later. He can't say, "Well that's a grey area and so I won't make a decision." Among other things, he is paid for making decisions. If he won't face up to this necessity, sooner or later he is an ex-manager. Continuing with right and wrong, there are nit-pickers who say there are no absolutes. These nit-pickers have lost sight of the fact that there are things that are predominately true. As we grow and learn as managers, we discover that though there is no single universal truth in managing, there are certain things that are predominately true and things that are predominately false and, stated in our earlier terms, things that are predominately right or wrong. There are right and wrong ways to manage as well as moral or ethical rights and wrongs.

A great advantage of having a set of beliefs codified within one is that a person can draw on them for making decisions. This enables a person to be consistent in a general sense. John Gardner, in one of his books, says that modern organizations, in order to succeed, must have managers whose decisions or whose behavior is predictable. If a manager's decisions cannot be predicted with some degree of success by his subordinates, or by his peers, the progress of the organization will suffer.

To conclude our comments on beliefs, we think there are certain areas where it is very advisable for every manager to have basic beliefs. Without attempting to climb into your mind and tell you how to think or what to think, we nevertheless suggest that your basic beliefs are not comprehensive unless they include the following areas:

1. What you think about people in general.
2. What you think about yourself, specifically.
3. What you think about your family.
4. What you think about your company.
5. What you think about your city and state.
6. What you think about your nation.
7. What you think about people reporting to you.
8. What you think about the boss you report to.
9. What you think about yourself as a teacher.
10. What you think about yourself as a leader.

What are your ambitions in all areas of your life, and do you *believe* you can achieve most of them?

Beliefs are the foundation of our basic attitudes. Our attitudes flow out of our conviction, our beliefs. We believe that attitudes are a great determinate as to how successful we are in our marriage, raising our children, serving our community, and in managing.

A young manager with *good attitudes* is well on his way toward becoming a successful manager. A new manager with poor attitudes has two strikes on him. The probability is he will fail or, at best, be a mediocre manager.

Every manager must be a planner, an organizer, a decision maker, and a person who gets things done. Managers get things done by and through others. If the manager can get things done due to his influence rather than because he exerts his power, he'll be—in this way, at least—a top-flight manager. Bosses are appointed; leaders earn the respect and confidence of the men and women they manage. They manage best who have many "right attitudes"—including MacGregor's Theory Y way of thinking about people. Theory Y holds that people do want to work, and that they want to do it right the first time. If they understand the confines of policy and procedure, they will produce at a high level. Not only that, but they gain satisfaction from a job well done. MacGregor's Theory X (not recommended) says that people are lazy and undependable and must be strongly directed—if not driven—otherwise production will be poor.

Let us make clear our attitude toward our target audience of young managers and those who aspire to become managers.

1. We look at you as individuals of dignity, merit, and worth.
2. We look at you as managers who can do good work.
3. We look at you as individuals who exercise a constructive influence on the society in which you live.
4. We look upon you as men and women who are above average and are willing to "pay the price" for above-average achievement.

What are some of the things that set you apart and make you members of a better-than-average group?

We expect that you are all (you new managers) well above average and superior individuals, thanks to your parents, and their teaching and the teaching of others and your own thinking that has led to acceptance of real values, and/or ethical standards, and/or a moral code, and/or something that sustains you, gives you courage, and enables you to rise above misfortune and contribute more than an average amount to all with whom you are associated. You generally have good and constructive attitudes.

Attitudes are huge in number and diverse in nature. We claim that the ones you accept and the ones you reject have much to do with your actions and success as a manager, and also as a citizen, and a family man or woman.

One attitude is "I can do."
Another is "I can't do."

One attitude is "I want to grow."
Another is "I don't want to grow," or "I can't grow."

One attitude is "promotions are based on merit."
Another is "You can't be promoted without luck and/or political drag."

One attitude is "I am largely the master of my destiny."
Another is "My life is governed by circumstances."

In each case the first attitude is the constructive one that characterizes many successful managers.

Summary

We suggest that you know clearly your beliefs. It is a good idea to write them down.

We believe that your attitudes flow out of your beliefs.

We are convinced that your attitudes affect your managing style.

We have concluded that your managing style affects the results you achieve.

Finally, we think your results are a measure of your success.

Query: As a young manager, if my beliefs and attitudes are A-OK, what else is important in managing better?

Answer: Chapters 2 through 11 cover many ideas that are useful to those who want to manage better.

Query: If my beliefs and attitudes don't make for business success, should I think them through and come up with an improved package of beliefs and attitudes?

Answer: Yes, if you can do so without compromising your integrity. Integrity is better than success achieved at the cost of a surrender of conscience.

I want for everyone a good life (their definition).
I am convinced that in one's total life, as well as in
one's business career, possession of most of the
seven characteristics listed on the next page are
essential. Anyone who finds himself lacking in any
of them except number 6 (average to superior
intelligence) can develop himself to the point that
such current deficiencies as exist can be and are
overcome.

Personal growth and development is a do-it-
yourself job, I think.

Paul M. Hammaker

I haven't seen many people succeed in achieving
their goals if they didn't want to. The world is not
structured to help the nonmotivated up the ladder of
success.

Louis T. Rader

2

Distinguishing attributes that many successful managers possess and use

Young managers often ask themselves—and some of them ask others—is there a formula for achieving business success? Are there certain characteristics or qualities that most successful managers possess and use?

The authors, after many years of personal contact with many successful managers, have concluded that the majority of successful managers do have seven qualities or traits. Individual managers may have many more, but the characteristics that most successful managers have in common are:

1. Self-motivation.
2. Emotional maturity.
3. Common sense and good judgment.
4. People sensitivity.
5. Inquiring minds.
6. Average to superior intelligence.
7. Integrity.

The first five characteristics can be learned and developed, while six and seven are less easily developed, but can be nourished. In fact, a type of nourishment for integrity is to develop sensitivity about ethical issues. Not all decisions relate only to economics—

many also involve ethical issues or problems. And so far as intelligence is concerned, most of us have far more mental capacity than we use. Managers we have known who achieved much with only average intelligence realized that the managerial job involved a balance among the six other factors listed.

Before discussing these qualities we will recap the points affecting young managers' success that have been made previously.

The clearer and sounder and more comprehensive a manager's beliefs are, the greater is his chance of achieving above average success.

A manager's beliefs at ages 25, 30, 35, 40 are not all the same. Men grow in scope and stature because of their increased perception and broadened perspective. A manager's beliefs at age 25 and 30 are the true basis of his character and actions. However, they may be only a hint of his character and actions 10 or 20 years later. Men grow, and beliefs can and do change.

Clear, sound beliefs are the basis of a manager's attitudes. The sounder his beliefs are, the better his attitudes will be.

A manager's behavior and performance and the results secured are affected greatly by his attitudes.

Managers, before they started to manage, had beliefs, attitudes, and a pattern of behavior; they also had traits or characteristics or qualities and—it is to be hoped—they included the seven we have mentioned.

The authors believe it is quite important for the young manager to know what the qualities are that make for success, to evaluate himself related to each one, and—if he detects a personal weakness in one or more—to build a program to strengthen himself where he is weak.

Both bosses and subordinates, though they may not go through a formal, analytical process, perceive the young manager's strengths or weaknesses in the seven areas or qualities mentioned. Since they do, it is only prudent for the young manager to have his own accurate perception and evaluation.

Does a young manager have to have every one of the seven attributes mentioned to be a successful manager?

No, but if he does not have most of them, he is not likely to achieve much success in the business of managing.

Self-motivation

In order to achieve the desires and objectives that most young managers have, as listed in Chapter 1, they must be self-motivated to work both hard and smartly. Such motivation is the driving force which turns their dreams or desires into reality. Self-motivation is the dynamic force that supplies the needed energy. Logic determines the direction into which that energy is channeled.

The high-accomplishment manager has a high degree of self-motivation. He wants to succeed—he knows all the reasons that he wants to, whether it be money, power, status, self-fulfillment, or whatever. Different people are motivated by different reasons, such as desire for success or fear of failure; a desire to give one's family all the advantages in the world, a desire for early retirement in order to travel.

The reasons for high self-motivation are secondary. The main point is that successful people have it, and it thus forms the driving force that supplies the willpower to achieve the desired results.

Success seems to intensify self-motivation. Repeated failure often dulls or even destroys it.

One readily observable manifestation of self-motivation is a high level of energy. A high energy level is commented on by many students of management as being a trait of the majority of successful managers from the lowest to the highest level of management. The successful are energetic. Their energy is apparent and seems to be appealing to their bosses and subordinates.

We have referred to motivation as a dynamic drive. That drive, capitalizing on good physical health, results in zest and energy. It is a force of attraction. It is attractive to most of the people young managers deal with.

Some say successful people are driven men in that they have high aspirations and high energy levels. It is almost obvious that people who are lethargic, apathetic, and low in energy are not likely to be above the average either in desire for accomplishment or in the realization of high objectives. This means that people of high accomplishment as a rule must and do have good physical health. They keep themselves in shape by exercising and relaxing. They know they cannot expend a high level of energy unless they can generate it by good health. They also know that good physical well-being begets good mental health. The Latin proverb states "Mens sano in corpore sano"—a healthy mind in a healthy body.

Young managers with a high energy level both work hard and play hard. Their high energy level assists them in working toward the top of their skill. In brief, a high energy level seems to be one means, along with strong self-motivation, to achieve personal growth, greater responsibility, and higher rewards.

Query: Do you have enough guts, self-motivation, to achieve your objectives?

Answer: If so, great. If you do not, then sooner or later you must reduce your aspirations and objectives or find a reason and a way to achieve stronger personal motivation.

Query: Can a young manager, if he isn't a self-starter, learn to motivate himself?

Query: As a result of self-motivation, can a young manager grow and develop?

Answers: If the answer to these two queries is no, then every manager who is not strongly motivated is stuck with himself as he is right now. He can expect no increase in his own personal self-motivation, nor can he expect to realize much personal growth and development. In addition, he cannot expect to improve substantially his skill in dealing with people. In brief, he is a static manager and the only thing that will happen to him in business is that he will grow older year by year and at best experience modest increases in responsibility and compensation.

We believe men who are not self-starters usually have the unexercised ability to achieve self-motivation that will enable them to aspire and achieve at levels noticeably higher than existed before they achieved strong self-motivation. Latent self-motivation can be changed into active self-motivation by a wife, a need to educate the children, the desire for a motor cruiser, and in many other ways.

An observation: Strong motivation plus average intelligence produces greater success than superior intelligence plus weak motivation.

Emotional maturity

This trait is probably the one that is most in evidence, either by its presence or absence, to all who come in contact with a person. It represents the degree of self-control which a person has; his self-insight; his tendency to act as an adult rather than as a child; for example, the acceptance of responsibility when results are not satisfactory, rather than blaming someone else. This, like so many personal characteristics, is derived from one's parents as well as from the environment. But a person who studies himself, who realizes what his temperament is, can modify and improve his behavior. He does not have to react to a critical situation as his father may have with explosive violence. He can develop a temperament of calm judgment which will make his peers and superiors credit him with emotional maturity.

It should be noted, however, that some managers deliberately develop planned anger in certain cases at certain times. They do this to impress on someone the magnitude of the error they or someone else has committed, and so it is primarily for effect. It is, unfortunately, true, however, that people who do this some-times get carried away with the technique and develop a habit of getting very mad. The net result is bad for all parties. A person who has good emotional stability does not get angry easily, does not blame others for his problems, and in general exudes a feeling of confidence.

Emotional maturity is expressed in stability of character. One who has this quality keeps his poise—he doesn't panic. He has self-control. He is in charge of himself and, because he is, is able to and does manage himself. He has a basis for managing others. A young manager possessing emotional maturity is self-disciplined, and because of this sets a tone that leads many of his subordinates to act in a disciplined and adult manner. All these simple yet valuable facets of emotional maturity help a young manager to manage effectively.

Emotional maturity is a quality of personality made up of a number of elements. It is stick-to-itiveness, the ability to stick to a job, to work on it, and to struggle through until it is finished, or until one has given all one has in the endeavor. It is the quality or capacity of giving more than is asked or required in a given situation. It is this characteristic that enables others to count on one—thus it is reliability.

Endurance enters into the concept of maturity; the endurance of difficulties, unpleasantness, discomfort, frustration, hardship. The ability to size things up, make one's own decisions, is a characteristic of maturity.

Usually, emotional maturity includes a determination, a will to succeed. Of course, maturity represents the capacity to cooperate; to work with others, to work in an organization and under authority. The mature person is flexible. He can show tolerance without abandoning his basic beliefs. He can be patient and, above all, he has the qualities of adaptability and compromise.

Successful young managers as a rule do not have as much emotional maturity as many older managers, but they do have a considerable degree of it.

Query: Can a young manager determine how much emotional maturity he has?

Query: Can a young manager increase the extent of his emotional maturity?

Answers: The young manager can list a few significant aspects of emotional maturity and evaluate himself on each. Also he can discover from trusted friends and family members where he stands. A few questions he might raise are:

1. How adult do I act?
2. Do I usually exercise self-control?
3. Do I have persistence, stick-to-itiveness?
4. Am I reliable?
5. Can I endure frustrations and still pursue and achieve my objectives?

In seeking the opinion of a trusted friend, instead of a direct approach such as, "Do you think I act as an adult?" he can say, "I believe two characteristics of adults are—"

1. They keep their poise; they don't panic.
2. They overcome obstacles and achieve their objectives.

Let's talk about someone you and I both know and determine how adult he is. This can go on into a comment by the young manager to his friend, "You certainly are a sound, sensible adult and that's one reason why I value your opinions." (Say this only if true.) It is likely the friend will sooner or later say something about the *adultness* of the young manager. This will be a clue as to the degree of emotional maturity the friend thinks the young manager possesses. This same technique can be used on the other four questions.

If a young manager determines that he needs to become more emotionally mature and wants to, he can lay out a program for this type of growth.

If the young manager wilts under pressure or when results are not up to standards, if he really doesn't see himself in an adult manner as being able to deal with pressure and accept full responsibility for results, then he has a problem. Three solutions are: (1) do nothing; (2) worry; (3) identify the causes and arrive at a specific program to correct his weaknesses.

Possible reasons for wilting under pressure are poor health, lack of vitality, an unwillingness to accept the fact that problems and difficulties are par for the course, and the lack of understanding that in the end individuals master their problems or become second-raters railing at circumstance and the unfairness of life and fate. Those who solve their problems are winners. Those who whine and blame others are, in the end, losers.

How does a young manager correct a lack of emotional maturity? One way is by reading the biographies of great men such as Benjamin Franklin, or history as discussed by Churchill or the Bible, or anything that shows the trials, tribulations, and accomplishments of men and women, living and dead. It can also be done by observing how others meet such situations. In the end he does it by adopting, really arriving at, convictions that flow into attitudes and behavior that are mature.

It is possible for a young professional to believe he is incapable of doing a good job when his superior knows the opposite. Mature individuals have confidence in their ability to cope. Here is an example of emotional immaturity: During World War II many engineering groups worked 6 days a week and 12 hours per day. The pressure was intense and there were casualties among the civilian population as well as among the military. A very competent young engineer who was designing large wind tunnel drives—40,000 horsepower—approached his supervisor one day to tell him that he didn't believe he was qualified to do the engineering design work and should be dropped down to an engineering assistant's job. The supervisor pooh-poohed the thought, told the man he was very capable (which he was), and to forget the whole thing. However, when the man showed up again a week later and quietly stated that he had been up to the roof of the building three times that morning trying to get up enough nerve to jump off, the supervisor really listened. The plant doctor recommended that the man be given the work he sought, essentially the same engineering calculation but without the final responsibility for performance, and it was done with little decrease in pay.

However, since this was not the first time a man had either cracked up or been on the verge, the supervisor asked the consulting psychiatrist if there were any clues which would warn him in advance. In essence, the psychiatrist's reply was that whenever a person who had been doing a good job tells you he can no longer cope with his problems, whether they be the job or his co-workers, his family, or his religion, the chances are that this lack of confidence, unless reversed, is the starting point of a breakdown. Another fairly certain indication is when an engineer who has been doing an adequate job, suddenly wants to be transferred to employee relations. "This occurs," said the consulting psychiatrist, "because the man believes he and others are being badly treated by nonsensitive supervisors, and if he were in employee relations he would see to it that the manager did develop people-sensitivity."

Common sense and good judgment

Common sense and good judgment are very difficult characteristics to describe, but they represent a very broad area on which judgments are made fast and easily by a young person's superior. If the young manager wears outlandish or off-beat or unusual clothes (by the prevailing standards of his firm), one of his superiors may comment, "He does not have good judgment." Or if he joins a protest march on a city street, even in a good cause, he may be tagged as not having common sense. Or if he

antagonizes secretaries or janitors or librarians by little idiosyncrasies, he may be said to be lacking in common sense. It
may be unfortunate, but it is true, that the criteria of what is
common sense is the standard of the critic—which may not be
just. But if the critic is the young manager's boss, it is nevertheless a real and important standard.

When a young designer was chided for something he had done
by his boss with the statement, "No one with any common
sense would have done that," the designer replied, "Mr. Black,
common sense is a gift of God and I merely have a technical
education." He might have added, though, that as he got more
experience it would contribute to his store of common sense and
improve his judgment.

Generally, however, people lacking in common sense stand out
in discussion groups by their completely impractical suggestions
which do not strike the hearers as creative thinking but as
hysterical ranting. So, on the one hand, the young manager
should be a creative thinker searching for novel approaches to
company problems but, on the other hand, these suggestions
cannot be so far divorced from what is possible that the young
manager is considered to be lacking in good judgment or
common sense.

Common sense may not be as common as the designation of
it as "common" suggests. If everyone acted in a common-sense
manner, the world in general and managers in particular would
have far fewer problems.

We have linked common sense and good judgment as being
characteristic of most successful young managers. They are,
though the extent of each is less than that of senior managers.
Common sense can and is developed more and more as managers
gain experience, and grow in perception. Likewise judgment, like
wine, usually improves with age. This improvement is greatest
in managers who grow in total stature—that is, become more
aware of all aspects of life and history and the current scene.
Voltaire said in effect, I refuse to discuss any matter or subject
until you have defined the terms. In that sense there follows our
definition of common sense and good judgment: "Common
sense" is what the people with whom the young manager is
associated consider to be reasonable and normal and "right,"

whether they are decisions, actions, general behavior, programs, or aspirations. "Good judgment" is exemplified by decisions and actions that are reasonable and acceptable to most or all parties of interest. Good judgment is based on observation, study, and experience. In a given situation, decision makers of good judgment usually arrive at similar or at least compatible answers and conclusions.

Query: If a young manager needs to add to his store of common sense, can he do so? If so, how?

Query: If a young manager aspires to be able to exercise better judgment, can he learn to? If so, how?

Answers: He can observe and, if necessary, write down what type of decisions and actions gain the approval of his boss. Also, in a more comprehensive way, he can list the behavior and ways of thinking that have widespread approval. These are not only acceptable but reflect the ideas of many as to what is sensible. Equally valuable is listing decisions and actions that are considered unacceptable or irresponsible or wrong. They represent group and general thinking as to things that are not sensible, or reasonable, or acceptable. Hence, one who does such things lacks common sense—in the group's view.

There are cases where the common-sense view is not correct, though they are rare. An extreme example of lack of common sense in the public view was the Wright brothers' conviction that they could build a machine that could fly.

All people, managers and workers and students, parents and children, old and young, are arriving at conclusions—that is to say, making judgments—day after day. An individual judges it won't rain, so he leaves the umbrella at home. A motorist's judgment is that other drivers will respect the red light. And so it goes. In general, good judgment is based on observation and experience and is exercised by weighing alternatives and then selecting the one that is most appropriate (related to objectives and standards) and realistic.

A young man who wants to improve his judgment in a limited sphere such as his own business, can learn by observation, by thoughtful consideration, by the results, by the opinions of others, what decisions led to actions that produced desirable results. Also, he can identify judgments that produced poor or undesirable results.

Though it is a great simplification, there is much pragmatic support for the statement that without good judgment in decision making and in implementation, good results are not achievable. This may be considered painfully obvious, yet many young managers in the early stages of their careers demonstrate a lack of common sense and good judgment. They don't understand or practice what critics would call the obvious.

There are some conclusions regarding running a business which are so elementary, or axiomatic, that the mere statement of them often makes people smile. They can be dismissed as being obvious, or just common sense. One of the authors started to put some of these together while he was a manager in the early 1960s as a means of emphasizing what he felt were principles which should never be forgotten. Their mere statement is often of value to emphasize points, or positions, for practitioner and student alike. Here is a summary of "Rader's Rules"—with comments on each rule below.

Rule 1.   Never run out of money or credit.
Rule 2.   The sum of all costs should be less than the amount of money received from the customer.
Rule 3.   You can't sell the second if you can't sell the first.
Rule 4.   When the quarterback says to go around left end, you go around left end.
Rule 5.   It doesn't matter how good your calculus is if your arithmetic is no good.
Rule 6.   Anybody off the street can run a business at a loss.
Rule 7.   Statistics are for losers.
Rule 8.   If you don't get the facts, the facts will get you.

Rule 1: The first law of business is, "Never run out of money or credit." If a company does so, it tends to lose the confidence of its vendors, of its employees, of its stockholders, of its customers, of its lenders and, indeed, of the public in general. When the quick asset ratio of current assets to current liabilities is calculated, the calculator and his bosses are paying attention to Rule 1.

It is not hard to run out of money. One of the most common methods is to spend too much on R&D. The scientist or engineer will always say, "But that is good money—well spent, and it's really an investment in the future and therefore you should put it into inventory not expense." A modification of the cliché about how businesses can go broke states there are now three ways: "Wine, women and engineers."

Moving into a new plant before the old one is completely utilized is another common cause for small businesses to run out of money and out of luck; and putting money into inventories and not aging receivables also takes its toll.

Rule 2: "The sum of all costs should be less than the amount of money received from the customer"—that is, less than the selling price. This appears obvious unless you have been in charge of a budget-making session. Each functional participant believes his work is more important than anybody else's and, therefore, requires more money to accomplish satisfactorily— always, of course, for the welfare of the company. This may be claimed for engineering, or marketing, or manufacturing. Taken together, these individual estimates of expenditure often exceed the total income. Therefore, agreement has to be obtained on lower expenditures, or the general manager must enforce a set of figures which obeys Rule 2. The participants must agree in principle that costs must be less than income. The general manager, in effect, says, "Don't argue with me, argue with the figures."

Rule 3: "You can't sell the second if you can't sell the first." In the early days of large computers no one wanted to buy the first for many reasons. There was no proof that computers worked, or that there was no software available, and if a computer did break down, there was no nearby machine on which to run the work. So the first machine was often a give-away—that is, sold at a massive discount so it could act as the backup for the second. These first machines were often sold to universities, for their scientific faculties knew that they could always make it work, or redesign and rebuild it if necessary. Their confidence may have bordered on foolhardiness, but it has been alleged that academicians are rarely inhibited by their own ignorance.

Rule 4: "When the quarterback says to go around left end, you go around left end." Even if the right side is open, a man who doesn't follow the signals won't be on the team long even if he scores the occasional touchdown. Why? Because he is not dependable.

Advice often given to subordinates who gripe about the signals called, is to the effect that "When you get to be president you can run the team your way, but till then do it the boss's way."

Rule 5: "It doesn't matter how good your calculus is if your arithmetic is no good." Management in the financial sphere consists usually of analyzing simple numbers, not equations, nor intersections of curves, nor extrapolations of future results. No amount of higher math, whether it be queing theory or linear programming or regression analyses, will help at all if the simple difference between income and outgo is negative. Simple arithmetic—addition and subtraction—without any great emphasis on the number of places to the right of the decimal is the key to common-sense accounting and management success.

Rule 6: "Anybody off the street can run a business at a loss." The woods are full of such people. It doesn't take a great deal of talent or aptitude or skill. And so people who run a business at a loss are not very valuable—even though they can prove in words that the loss was inevitable and beyond anybody's control.

Rule 7: "Statistics are for losers." To talk in terms of first downs when there are no points given for downs is to beg the question. The payoff is in results, not effort.

Rule 8: "If you don't get the facts, the facts will get you." This is a favorite saying of Abe Zarem, consultant and former vice president of Xerox, who built and sold a business to them. He goes on to say, "Nothing is more tragic in this life than the murder of beautiful theories by ugly facts."

People sensitivity

Most successful managers are aware of the fact that just as their people are dependent on them, they are dependent on their

people. A working-managing situation is one of mutual dependence. This can be stated:

$$\text{Good Boss} + \text{Poor Workers} = \text{Poor Result}$$
$$\text{Poor Boss} + \text{Good Workers} = \text{Fair Result}$$
$$\text{Good Boss} + \text{Good Workers} = \text{Good Result}$$

The boss is dependent on the workers—the workers are dependent
on the boss.

It is difficult to determine what the rank order is of the big
seven attributes that most successful managers possess and use,
since they go together and form a cohesive and unified whole.
The subtraction of any one is serious. The absence of any two
or three probably means the difference between somewhat con-
spicuous and mediocre success. Nonetheless, the importance of
people sensitivity is extremely great. It—people sense, people
understanding, people developing, people satisfying—can overcome considerable deficiencies in emotional maturity and even
of common sense and good judgment, as well as some lack of
intelligence.

A few of the questions that the people-sensitive manager
knows the answers to are:

What are my people like?
What makes them tick?
What do they want?
How will they react?
How can I make their goals and the goals of the company
reasonably compatible?
How can I help them grow?
How can I create a climate that will produce personal satisfac-
tion and good business results?

This suggests that the young manager should like people, be
interested in them, enjoy challenge, be a psychologist, and a
leader. This is a good summary of some of the requisites for
managing people successfully.

Of course, a young manager needs to understand his business
and his responsibility, be able to identify and solve problems, be
able to identify and capitalize on opportunities, and be able to

manage in a way that suits his beliefs and personality and is acceptable to his people.

Clearly, a young manager needs to be able to achieve a good batting average in selecting people, in training them, in helping them to achieve their goals, in rewarding superior performance, and in penalizing poor efforts, poor results, failures.

People react negatively to a vacillating, uncertain, indecisive, fearful boss. It follows that young managers should be decisive, confident, and courageous.

Many young managers who are destined for greater-than average success practice management by objectives, which the workers set and he approves or which are jointly arrived at.

People-people-people are the world of the young manager. As an interested student of people, as a thoughtful practitioner of leadership, the young manager can establish a foundation and record that will lead to increased responsibility, status, compensation, success and satisfaction.

Most people like to be team members and people-sensitive managers know this. The following example of a European manager emphasizes the importance of this people sensitivity. The manager had just spent a year in the United States at parent company headquarters. He told us, "I learned two things in the United States: First, never to use the pronoun, 'I,' but to use 'we'; never, 'I did it,' but 'we did it'; not, 'my budget,' but 'our budget.'"

"The second thing I learned, was not to be afraid to say, 'I don't know.' In Europe it is considered demeaning to ever admit you don't know, especially if you are the general manager. In the United States, no one is afraid to say, 'I don't know,' and it certainly speeds up the discussions. Little or no fancy dancing around goes on here to save face, and a great deal more is accomplished in the same time."

Inquiring minds

The most successful managers we have known through the years have had inquiring minds. Generally speaking, they were curious. They searched for better ways to manufacture or sell or control or to reduce cost or to increase margins or to improve quality and reliability or to stimulate people or to conceive and develop new products. Young managers, headed for growth and success, are searchers after more knowledge about their particular responsibility, about their company, and about their industry. They have an idea that someone else may be doing something a little better and they want to learn the why and how of this.

One way inquiring minds, alert minds, keep abreast of what's going on is by reading *The Wall Street Journal, Business Week,* and the trade magazines or papers dealing with their industry. Since acquisition of information is frequently through reading, speed reading as taught by Evelyn Woods can be valuable. In addition to reading and observing, a good way for a young manager to learn more about his business is through contact with other areas of his own concern, including people in functions different from his own.

Part of many young managers' search for improvement can be, how can I become a more effective speaker? If this is a weak area, such a course as Dale Carnegie's can be of value to a young manager.

One big reason managers keep alert and curious is that it brings before them new ideas, provocative thoughts, and helps them arrive at better ways to think, analyze, decide, and act. One way to avoid boredom, smugness, and self-satisfaction is to have and use an alert, active, inquiring mind.

Managers frequently are forced to make decisions without complete information. They have to make decisions in times of uncertainty. All other things being equal, the alert, inquiring mind has accumulated and has available a better store of knowledge, a better set of ideas, and most likely a better ability to conjure up and evaluate practical alternative solutions to a problem than a manager who is simply doing his job and not making his innate curiosity a vehicle for personal growth and development.

Young managers, in the authors' view, should be actively curious, alert, and persistently seeking more information so as they progress upward they have an increasingly larger store of information, knowledge, and successful techniques, and hence become better equipped to cope with their present and future responsibilities. Ultimately, they can become uniformly well-informed in many diverse fields such as government actions, foreign government regulations, pricing philosophy of competitors, national economic conditions, trends in the commodity markets, and the newest as well as the best thinking in management development, or whatever. Such managers are always curious, always seeking new ideas, or willing to discuss the possibility of modifying old concepts to make them more valuable.

An inquiring mind is not only valuable as a business asset, it is, the authors think, fun and satisfying to become a recognized expert or authority. Young managers are not experts, but they can lay the foundation for becoming masters of their trade or function or specialty later.

The natural reaction of many professionals is to criticize a new idea. The manager can create a climate by his behavior or written procedures that encourages minds to be inquiring and stimulates creativity. For example, the supervisor of a large development component was faced with the management of a very creative, versatile, and usually fast-responding professionals. He believed in brainstorming as an approach, but soon noticed that whenever a new idea was put forward, the almost automatic reaction of the rest of the brainy group was to point out its deficiencies. Accordingly, he initiated a simple rule. When a new idea was presented, a discusser must first elaborate on some of the possible positive features of the idea before he pointed out any shortcomings. If he did the latter first, he owed everybody at the meeting a dollar. It was truly amazing how, in a short time, all new ideas were positively treated, giving rise to many more new ones, and with consequent good results.

Average to superior intelligence

Young managers, senior managers, most managers are not stupid. Stupidity, when recognized, almost automatically bars an individual from entering the ranks of management.

Young managers must possess average intelligence or more. Our observation is that the vast majority of young managers do have at least average intelligence.

Whether or not grades in colleges and universities are an accurate reflection of intelligence is a subject of debate. The authors believe that a significant factor in grades is motivation. Highly-motivated average intelligence is often rewarded with higher grades than bored, uninterested, superior intelligence that secures passing grades with little effort. In any event, there have been many studies searching for a correlation between high grades in college and business success. No such relationship has been found. There seems to be as much data saying that the *C* man may do as well as the *A* student if he is willing to work as hard or harder than his competitor. Certainly "common sense" says that a person of superior intelligence, all other things being equal, should have a higher probability of success than one of lower capabilities. However, grades do not necessarily identify differences in intelligence and, in addition, all other things are rarely equal. How hard a person is willing to work, how smartly he works, and how well he gets along with people may be and often are as important as intellectual capability. It is true, however, that the job of a senior manager often includes so many diverse and varied matters that the more intelligence a person is endowed with, the more easily he should be able to comprehend the various facets of the job, and analyze and synthesize courses of action.

However, more than comprehension is required. Certainly, as between average and superior intelligence, the degree of excellence in such factors as motivation, emotional maturity, and good judgment are bound to be important. As mentioned, average intelligence plus strong self-motivation usually produces a better result than does superior intelligence and weak motivation.

The authors' sole conclusion here is that average intelligence is a must for successful managing. However, given average intelligence or more, the issue facing young managers is, how much of their mental power do they use?

Young managers (indeed, everyone) have four mental powers. They are:

1. The power to observe.
2. The power to retain (memory).

3. The power to analyze, criticize, and think logically (the power to reason).
4. The power to dream, imagine, conceive and visualize (creative thinking or creativity).

Related to the first power, an example of observation and also of experimentation occurred in the 16th century when Galileo decided to find out for himself what happened when he dropped a heavy and a light cannonball from the Leaning Tower of Pisa. Starting with Aristotle and for 2,000 years, it had been believed that heavy objects fell faster than light ones. Indeed, it was believed that a weight three times as heavy as another one fell three times as fast. The amazing result of Galileo's experiment was that both cannonballs, the heavy and the light one, hit the ground at the same time.

Rosser Reeves in *Reality in Advertising* wrote concerning this: "What Galileo demonstrated was not so much a fact about falling weights, as a new problem-solving method . . . based not on the authority of age and prestige but rather on the authenticity of current first-hand experimentation and observation."

Fuller utilization of the four mental powers is a type of growth. We believe that fuller utilization of these mental powers enables one to manage better. Some psychologists believe that most adults customarily use less than 20 percent of their brain's capacity. If managers are strongly motivated, place greater demands on themselves, and tap more of their mental capacity, then perhaps they use around 40 percent of their mental power. If so, their untapped capacity is 60 percent.

Part of the answer to achieving greater business success and personal satisfaction is not only to tap more of your mental potential, but also to realize more fully your potential as a whole man or woman in all of the other areas of your life and personality. An example of a dimension beyond the mental is the area of your basic beliefs. Your thoughts about people, and how to manage, rest on how you look at mankind and your attitudes concerning other human beings.

As discussed, these things have much to do with the degree of success managers achieve. To date we have said:

1. Clear, sound, comprehensive beliefs are possessed by most successful managers.
2. Constructive attitudes flow out of such convictions/beliefs and lay a good foundation for managing successfully.
3. Most successful managers have most or all of seven traits or qualities.
4. Self-motivation and emotional maturity and good judgment, plus average to superior intelligence, are four of the *big seven.*

Integrity

People trust their careers and compensation and work-a-day satisfaction to their boss. They have no option except to go to another concern where they'll find a new boss, or to leave the work force, or to graduate into the management ranks. Since people do the work, and since they can perform at higher or lower levels, their attitudes toward the boss are as significant as his attitudes toward them.

Workers like an honest, trustworthy, dependable, predictable boss who is fair, interested, and will when necessary fight to defend their interests and to gain for them deserved rewards. Workers come to detest a boss who is unreliable, dishonest, not on the level, and lacks integrity.

If a manager does not have basic integrity or honesty, he cannot hide it from his subordinates and peers. If the workers mistrust their manager, are not sure he tells the truth, are not certain that he puts the section or department or division's welfare ahead of his own, then their performance and the team's are bound to suffer.

Beyond honesty and saying what you mean and being reasonably consistent and on the level, is the quality of ethical behavior. Ethical behavior is acting in ways that the group, the company, the public think a manager ought to act. This goes well beyond simple honesty and integrity. The interest in ethics and ethical behavior is growing. As a prediction, the authors believe that high ethical standards and consistent ethical behavior will become one of the more important measures in the future of managers, young and old.

The following is quoted from a talk on ethics and the businessman given by Paul Hammaker to an annual meeting of the Virginia State Chamber of Commerce:

It is a real pleasure to have the opportunity to talk with you about ethics and the businessman. I am *for* both ethics and businessmen. We all have pretty clear and comprehensive ideas about business and businessmen, but are we equally clear about ethics?

Vernon Bourke of St. Louis University defined ethics as "the systematic study of human actions from the viewpoint of their rightness or wrongness as a means for the achievement of ultimate happiness."

Beyond this is the idea that people—individuals—want to be happy. It has been said the pursuit of happiness is the original stimulus for all human action. That may be an overstatement, but most individuals I know are keenly interested in the achieving of happiness. I believe the possession and practice of high ethical standards as a way of life leads to personal satisfaction and happiness.

A different statement on ethics was made by the late Dr. Albert Schweitzer. He said: "In a general sense, ethics is the name we give to our concern for good behavior. We feel an obligation to consider not only our own personal well being but also that of others and of human society as a whole."

Frederick Nolting, Jr., whom I believe many of you know and who is now teaching and dealing with ethics in our own [University of Virginia's] graduate business school, thinks the essence of ethical behavior is honesty. He also thinks that our university's honor system is based on simple, understandable, enforceable, ethical ideas. As you know, the honor code is based on students *not* lying, cheating, stealing. The system is student-run and it works!

Raymond Baumhard, president of Loyola University, conducted a landmark survey dealing with ethics and businessmen. Some definitions given by the businessmen he surveyed are:

Ethical means what my feelings (my conscience) tells me is right.
Ethical means acting in accord with my religious beliefs.
Ethical means to practice the "Golden Rule."
An objective definition is "what society considers fair and honest."
A subjective definition is "that which best serves my interest without harming others."

Now let's consider a definition of ethics from Bruce Henderson of the Boston Consulting Group: "Ethics is a self-imposed control of aspects of behavior. These aspects are always those actions which sacrifice self-interest for social benefit to others. There are no ethical issues for the lone castaway of an unpopulated island. Ethics represent the conflict between social norms and individual self-interest."

For the purpose of this talk and subsequent discussion, I am defining ethics as what men and women think they *ought to do*.

As we consider ethical issues, I believe most of us discover that we are faced by three areas: what we know we ought to do; what we know we ought not do; a grey area which often embraces a portion of the first and some of the second.

How do we, as executives, deal with the grey areas in our business considerations and decisions? A good way is to sort out the interests of the groups to be affected. A tried and true dilemma is, should a chief executive officer (CEO), decide to move his plant 1,000 miles to a better total economic climate that will enable his company to produce better earnings? Issue: Stockholders will benefit but local workers and local tax receipts will be injured temporarily or permanently. Ought the CEO work for the benefit of stockholders? Yes! Ought the CEO act in a way that hurts production workers and a community? No! So, if the CEO moves this plant, has he acted both ethically and unethically? If the CEO doesn't move the plant, is he being both ethical and unethical?

Recently Arjay Miller of Stanford suggested an interesting guideline for decision making: "Would you be comfortable if you heard your decision announced, explained, discussed and critically evaluated on TV?"

Part of the problem of what businessmen ought to do revolves around the public's definition of ethics or ethical behavior, or what the public believes business ought to do.

Businessmen usually think as economists and profitmakers and as managers responsible to stockholders. This is a good line of reasoning, but it isn't adequate today. Businessmen must think more than they have in social and political terms. For example, the recent so-called windfall profits of the major oil companies were OK in an economic sense. On the other hand, the timing of those profits was extremely unfortunate and the oil companies in retrospect would have been much better off, I believe, if they had limited their profits during this particular period. I suspect there was enough knowledge and time so that some action could have been taken to hold down profits. This would have been, let us say, bad immediate economics and good long-run politics. It also would have met the public's definition of business ethics—namely, what business ought to do. Since polls show that more than half those interviewed believe the oil companies contrived the shortage or didn't level with the public or took unfair advantage of the public, the issue is: Were the major oil companies ethical? If you leave it to popular opinion, they were not ethical. If you believe, as many people do, that Senator Jackson attempted to and succeeded in making a scapegoat of the major oil companies, how does this square with the facts, and was Senator Jackson acting in an ethical or unethical manner?

[Let me] express a few thoughts about Virginia. In the early days of this country, Virginia exercised great leadership in social, political, and ethical thought and actions. An example is the Declaration of Independence, which we regard as a great social, political, and ethical document. Since my definition of ethics deals with *ought to* and *ought not*, it is interesting to note that the Declaration is specific as to some 28 *ought not to be's*, which it calls injuries or usurpations.

Query: Can a manager live up to his own ethical standards and be successful in business?

Answer: Yes. We know many ethical, successful managers. Beyond that we believe that if a manager elects to act unethically by his own standards and is a sensitive individual, he will come to regret his unethical action regardless of the success he achieves. One of the participants in the Darden School's Executive Program said:

In 1962 I was promoted to sales engineer for my company. Never will I forget the words of our president: "Be honest and sincere with your prospects and customers." For 13 years I traveled and attempted to build a reputation on this philosophy for my company. If my company failed to meet a shipping promise, had a quality problem or other problems, I would personally call on my customers and tell them exactly what had happened. Never did I attempt to make up an excuse or white lie to cover up for something that happened in the plant.

Today, that president is retired from our company but you will find his philosophy of being honest and sincere still entrenched very deeply in the majority of the managers in our company. I am confident that this has had a lot to do with the unusual growth that we have had. All of our customers and even competition respects us for the way we do business.

An unknown author with a knack for stating desirable management traits concisely raised most of the following 42 questions that relate to the *big seven* attributes. The authors know that many of them are often asked about managers who are being considered for promotion. Here they are:

1. Is he energetic and is he dynamic in his attitude toward responsibilities?
2. Does he have capacity for hard work?

3. Is he capable of sustained effort without giving way to fatigue?

These are questions that can be answered favorably—that is, affirmatively—concerning young managers who are self-motivated and have a high energy level. They deal with no. 1 of the big seven—self-motivation. Some more questions follow:

4. Is he mature in his thinking and his bearing and is he emotionally stable?
5. Has he the capacity for impersonal and independent thinking without regard to self-serving influence exerted by others?
6. Is he open-minded and unprejudiced toward new ideas?
7. Does he accept criticism gracefully?
8. Does he have a judicious temperament; that is, does he habitually arrive at conclusions by logical processes regardless of his personal bias?
9. Is he objective?
10. Is he even-tempered, not giving way readily to moods and to worry about matters beyond his control?
11. Is he optimistic in attacking a new problem or does he tend to be deterred by difficulties?
12. Does he habitually inspire faith in his ability and inspire confidence in others?
13. Is he resourceful and persevering in the face of difficulties or does he give up easily?

Question nos. 4 through 13 deal with no. 2 in the big seven—emotional maturity. Most or all of them can be answered affirmatively—that is, favorably—if the young manager being considered for promotion is emotionally mature. The next questions can be answered in favor of the prospect for promotion who is A-OK in no. 3 of the big seven—common sense and good judgment.

14. Has he good judgment?
15. Does he have savvy?
16. What do his people think about him and his ideas?

The questions about intelligence are usually few in number, since adequate intelligence is assumed. However, on occasion a boss will ask concerning a young manager up for promotion:

17. Is he bright?
18. Is he smart?
19. Has he the mental capacity to do the job?

If the young manager has ordinary intelligence and strong motivation, the answers to these and similar questions are yes.

The following questions deal with no. 7 of the big seven—integrity.

20. Does he discriminate clearly between what he conceives to be right and wrong actions?
21. Does he persist in doing what he considers to be right, or does he succumb readily under stress?
22. Will he fight for a principle, even when he knows he represents an unpopular point of view?
23. Is he inclined to govern his conduct by principle rather than by expediency?
24. Is he sufficiently flexible to yield in detail without compromising on principle?
25. Is he reliable and dependable in meeting obligations to others?

Young managers of integrity score high on such questions.

Questions about no. 4 of the big seven—people sensitivity—are usually simple, such as:

26. Does he have a feel for people?
27. Do his people believe in him and respect him?
28. Does he help his people grow?
29. Is one of his strongest points dealing with people?
30. What weaknesses does he have in his relationship with his people?
31. What do his associates at his level think of him?
32. Do senior managers know him? If so, what do they think of him?

The young manager has created by his attitudes and actions the answers to nos. 26 through 30. His "public relations" largely provide the answer to questions 31 and 32. Number 5 in the big seven is the inquiring mind. Some questions asked in this regard are:

33. Is he well-informed on general business and economic trends, and can he discuss such problems confidently?
34. Can he detect spurious economic reasoning without losing intellectual objectivity?
35. Can he recognize economic and political trends and their implications for the business, and can he adapt his thinking to forces which he may abhor, but which cannot be avoided?
36. Is he well-informed about other external factors influencing the company's business, particularly how the company fits into the general setting of industry?
37. Is he interested in the nature of markets, sources of supply, and the competition of the company?
38. Is he well-informed about the company's competitive position, possibilities of growth and improvement, and how, in general, growth might be accomplished?
39. Is he studious and curious?
40. Does he habitually learn more than the job demands of him?
41. Is he aware of the increasing importance of legislation on economic life?
42. Does he in general keep informed about governmental regulations affecting the business and does he show reasonable capacity for analysis of such problems?

Questions 34, 36, 37, 39 and 40 are particularly appropriate for a young manager up for promotion. However, later on, as he progresses, the answers to questions 33, 35, 38, 41, and 42 become increasingly pertinent.

Questions for the reader

1. What are the *big seven?*
2. What is your own personal statement about each?
3. Do you want to subtract from what the authors have said? If so, what do you have to say?

4. Do you want to add to the authors' big seven? If so, what do you want to add and why?
5. Are the matters covered in Chapters 1 and 2, when believed and practiced, enough to make a manager successful?
6. Can a young manager design and implement a career plan for himself?

Managers are dependent on the people who
report to them. These people want a manager with
people-sensitivity and leadership ability who on a
cooperative basis achieves above average results for
his unit, section, department, division, or company.

Your people want to be important members of a
winning team. That is psychic pay—beyond the fair
money compensation they earn. I have never met
anyone who was not appreciative of truly deserved
and graciously given psychic pay.

Paul M. Hammaker

It's just as simple as this—if people like you for
whatever reason, they will help you, and if they
don't, again, for whatever reason, they will not help
you.

Louis T. Rader

3

*Managing principle
number one: Understand
who you are managing
through a knowledge of
and feeling for people*

This chapter and the next six cover what we believe to be the
basic areas with which management must be concerned. The
authors have worked in industry for a combined total of 70
years and have helped to manage businesses from small to very
large. In our operating days, although we took management
courses and seminars, read management articles and books, we
did not concern ourselves primarily with the principles underlying our actions, but with achieving the desired results.

After entering the academic areas, however, we have tried to
consolidate our beliefs and principles regarding managing and we
have been aided by the kinds of questions asked by graduate
students in the business school, questions such as:

Just what does management consist of?
Can management principles be taught?
What courses can I take which will make me a good manager?
Is management really a science or is it an art?
I know the fundamental definition of a manager is—one who
gets results through people—but what is there beyond that?
Is good managerial ability something one has to be born with, or
can it be developed?

There are naturally many possible answers to these kinds of questions. To some extent, management is an art but to a greater extent it has many of the attributes of a science. There is a large body of knowledge available concerning management principles, techniques, and skill. There are many theories of management. Assuming that the person who asks the above questions is himself a college graduate or equivalent, one approach to some answers is to look at the curricula of graduate schools of business that deal with business management. These generally cover with mandatory or optional courses subjects such as accounting, finance, control, marketing, operations, organizational behavior, quantitative analysis, business policy, the business environment, advertising, employee relations, labor relations, managerial behavior, statistical analysis, interpersonal behavior, and marketing research. Within each of these and other subject areas there is a great deal of both practical and theoretical information. In some schools (such as Harvard and the University of Virginia) the teaching is done primarily through the use of real cases. However, in the majority of business schools, courses are given in conventional lecture style, usually with a course textbook and/or readings.

Nearly all graduate schools of business offer short courses of from a few days' to 16 weeks' duration for practicing businessmen. These courses usually stress those aspects of management which are uppermost in peoples' minds as of the date the courses are given, or they discuss new concepts which may be gaining in popularity. Some examples might be acquisition or divestment analysis, new government regulations, ethics for the businessman, and transactional analysis.

Another approach to management training is used by General Electric. When GE in the early 1950s decided to establish its own management school, it was partly because it felt the existing business schools could not adequately serve its needs. GE established its own high-level study teams which reviewed all management literature and then wrote their own curriculum. The course was originally 13 weeks and later became a 10-week course given at GE's facility in Crotonville, New York. The participants were middle and upper management, most of whom had never had any formal management training but who were either in managerial jobs or being considered for such a job. The fundamental point here is that GE chose to teach management (and still does) not under the functional approach used by business schools, but under four major headings. These are planning, organization, integration, and measurement. It is GE's conviction that most of the essentials of management can be covered by these four major categories.

The American Management Association offers a large number of excellent courses to its members. Some of these are offered as part of a symposium or colloquium, or as a short course. One such course offered frequently is a one-week course called "Management Course for Presidents." The areas covered under the general title of "Basic Principles of Management" are planning, organization, control, climate, and leadership. In addition, other topics are often discussed, such as management ethics and the challenges facing management.

Richard Fear, formerly vice president of the Psychological Corporation, New York, and an eminently qualified industrial psychologist, has written a book which contains (in addition to very valuable down-to-earth guides on interviewing prospective employees) some very practical observations on management. These latter are derived from thousands of actual in-depth interviews and summarize the results of the author's practical experience. Fear states that in general the qualifications for the executive may be broken down into just two categories: (1) leadership and (2) administrative ability. Extrapolating these categories of Fear's into basic principles of management yields under leadership the ability to lead, motivate, and direct people to accomplish necessary results. Or, alternatively stated, one of the required areas of management expertise is a real knowledge of the human element—people. Similarly, under administrative ability the required areas of management expertise include short-range and long-range planning, oral and written communications, and a good general background which contributes to one's ability to see the overall picture.

In contrast to GE and AMA, business schools in general teach that the basics of management are best learned by studying the theory and practice of functional areas such as marketing, production, finance, and personnel, together with some training in communications, analysis of the external environment, and business policy. A major criticism frequently made of this kind of curriculum is that it usually is pitched at a high level and deals with problems and situations which the young Master of Business Administration (MBA) graduate is not likely to encounter until perhaps ten or more years after graduation. This is one of the prime reasons the authors believed the bright, aggressive young graduate is so often disillusioned with his first or second job.

Management courses given by graduate schools to businessmen and by companies such as AT&T or GE to their employees can do and pitch the courses to a well-identified audience—their own selectees. The problems dealt with and solutions arrived at are close to the real-life experience and needs of the businessmen attending. The usefulness of such courses is demonstrated by their continued support by business firms.

The above approaches to management training identify, literally, dozens of subject areas which the aspiring managers must master in order to be successful. Our belief is that these can be summarized into seven managing principles, and these form the subject of this and the following six chapters. A discussion dealing with the first area and the first principle follows.

Understanding who you are managing through a knowledge of and a feel for people

There is no principle of greater importance to young managers than understanding their people. This means knowing their people, knowing their hopes, aspirations, and objectives; their strengths and weaknesses; knowing what they want and what is important to them. This must be coupled with what the young manager thinks is important and what he wishes to accomplish. The combination becomes the basis for motivating and managing.

Most good managers are people-oriented. This is the observation of and conclusion of the authors, who have seen hundreds of managers in action. People-skill will be even more important in the future, we think. Tomorrow's successful managers will be both sensitive to people—really sensitive—and also results-oriented.

Query: Can I learn to manage and to lead?

Answer: Yes. As a manager you can learn to lead people—serve their needs—serve your company's needs and thereby be a socially useful as well as a successful manager. This is true for almost all managers if they want to, *really* want to! This is a relationship of *mutual dependence.* You as a manager are dependent for success on your people. They depend on you for leadership, support, recognition, and reward.

Mutual dependence means that to realize your expectations and hopes you have to depend on your people. They have their hopes and goals, and they expect you, their manager, to play a key role in helping them achieve their goals.

As a functioning manager, we expect you would have no difficulty spelling out point by point what you expect from the people who report to you. You have expectations—your people have expectations. When these are melded together in such a way that they are practical—yet not *easy* to achieve—and when, through cooperation, the desired results are forthcoming, then each party to the implied contract is satisfied. Not only are your people satisfied, but they find pride in their work and are happy in the association with you and the company. If you as a boss are not happy in your association with your people and the company, you better find out what the problem is. Some things that might be involved are:

1. You don't have clear-cut objectives.
2. You are not sure of your own bosses' expectations.
3. You can't seem to motivate people to produce satisfactory or superior results.
4. You are dissatisfied with working conditions or the company's product.
5. You are not sure your own best interests are tied to the company's best interests.

John Donne said something about mutual dependence several centuries ago: "No man is an island." Clearly this means that as one individual we are not alone but, indeed, are surrounded by many people. It also means that an individual is not self-sufficient but is dependent on others for many things. The world that you as a manager live in both at work and away from work is peopled by many other individuals. Your business success depends in a significant measure on how well you like, understand, and can lead your people.

While this book is concerned primarily with managing and your work, both of these are affected not only by your beliefs and attitudes (discussed in Chapter 1), but also by the net effect of your relationships with all kinds of people outside of the business. For instance, married men and/or women who are serving as managers are affected to an important degree by their wife or husband. In fact, marriage itself is a splendid example of mutual dependence. We think it is clear that when a man and woman enter into marriage and each is determined to be 100 percent independent, this goal in itself is impossible. Marriage is a cooperative venture and if each party is going to maintain individual rights and independence—and there is little understanding and little compromise, flexibility, and cooperation—then the marriage simply won't work. Such a marriage fails because the "partners" lack a knowledge of and a real feel for each other. They lacked people sensitivity and/or people skill.

It has been demonstrated to the authors' satisfaction many times that an understanding wife represents great support to a male manager. By the same token, when the woman of the household is the executive in business, her performance is influenced favorably to the extent that her husband is understanding and supportive of her efforts.

We know as do you that there are many types of people relationships out of business, beyond that of marriage. These involve technical associations, such as engineering societies, social societies such as the Elks, societies existing within a church as well as the church itself, civic groups such as the Rotary, and membership in sports groups such as bowling teams. All of these relationships add to or subtract from the manager's ability to manage. If he has people trouble in out-of-business situations, he is likely to have people trouble in business. If, on the other hand, he gets along well with people in the various out-of-business groups mentioned, and deals with the individuals in them in a manner that earns their confidence and respect, then this same characteristic is likely to carry over into his business life and increase the probability that he will be a successful manager.

Recently one of the authors was going from the Newark Airport into Manhattan on a bus driven by a man who seemed old and almost decrepit, if not senile. It was with great surprise that the author noted that with each stop, whether at a tollgate or held up on a bridge, the driver had a personal word to say to each of the attendants. He called one "Mike," one "Bill," and made a thoughtful inquiry or an appropriate remark to each of them. In turn, they said to him, "We missed seeing you. How are you doing?" or, "What about that son of yours? How is he?" This homey incident is illustrative of a man who is not a manager but who has a great feel for people and has developed rapport with the attendants he meets in the course of his duties. His underlying attitude apparently is one of friendliness and he seemed to believe that a little courtesy, politeness, and human kindness makes life better for everyone. We think we all know within ourselves that the kind of attitude this bus driver demonstrated toward people represents a great asset in each manager's dealings with people within or without his business.

It is abundantly clear—and the more we observe and learn, the truer it seems to be—that a basic principle of managing is dealing effectively with people. The function of a manager is to accomplish results by talking, guiding, assisting, and leading other people to achieve the desired results. Most successful managers know how to deal effectively with those reporting to him or her and with the echelon of management above them. No manager achieves much unless he is:

1. Good at selecting good people.
2. Good at assisting his or her people to grow and develop.
3. Good at dealing with his or her people fairly and persuasively.
4. Good at setting standards—high standards—for performance and continually insisting on achievement of the planned and required results.
5. Good at rewarding superior performance and penalizing those whose performance is subpar.

On selecting good people

Query: What if a young manager says, "I don't have the gift of choosing good people"?

Answer: So far as selecting good people is concerned, this is something that most managers can learn to do if they put their mind to it. One thing to do is to look at the track record of the person being considered. Has he done well in his present and previous work? Has his performance been improving or declining? If he wasn't good in his previous work, why do you think he would be good when he reports to you? If he hasn't been a hard worker in his present job, why would he work hard for you? If he is to be hired from the outside, get some references and personally talk with each of them to see what they have to say about the prospect. If he works in your company, talk to several people who work with him and find out what they think are his strengths and weaknesses.

Two very successful young presidents we know have interesting ideas on selecting people. One of them (whose business has grown in sales from $4,000,000 to over $40,000,000 in seven years) is interested in hiring men for store managers who have what he calls "high economic value." His criteria for selecting potential managers include:

Health	Family situation
Age	Education
Appearance	Integrity
Human behavior	Personal goals
Intelligence	Personal values

His corporate objectives which he discusses with a prospective employee are: be moral; produce goods or services for mankind; contribute to society; earn a 20 percent return on investment.

After this president explains corporate objectives, he asks the prospective employee to define his personal objectives. The president asks himself, do the two sets of objectives "fit"? If not, he does not hire the prospect.

This young president says that man has six predominate values. (All six are discussed in Chapter 11.) One of them is: economic, meaning practical, interested in getting results and gaining personal wealth. Economic man wants to do useful work and be well-compensated for doing it in a satisfactory manner. That's the kind of man this president wants.

The young president, through the job interview, forms an impression of the prospect in many ways. If it is his conclusion that the man places a low value on the economic, this president believes if the person were hired and given dollar incentives the person couldn't care less. Hence, the president selects people only with high economic value.

The second president, Harry E. Figgie, Jr. of Automatic Sprinkler Corporation of America (ATO), took, by internal growth and acquisition, a company with $20,000,000 in sales initially to over $350,000,000 in sales in ten years. He says:

> I spend more time on personnel than anything else I do. Every man who joins our corporation is tested to make sure that his mental capacity ranks in the top 10 percent of the college population. Every salesman, every industrial engineer, and every man up for a promotion must be interviewed by several persons, including a final interview with me.
>
> I spend many of my weekends interviewing men. We found that three things must be present in a man if he is to be a success in an operating capacity in a manufacturing company. *One is just plain mental alacrity— intelligence.* You know there are several types of intelligence. You can measure one and possibly two, but mental alacrity is the only type you can really measure. We say a man has to have three things: *mental alacrity, drive,* and *sensitivity.* If he lacks any one of these things, you've got real trouble. You get a man who has drive and no sensitivity or intelligence and he'll walk right through that wall. You get a man with intelligence and sensitivity with no drive and he'll cower in the corner. We've really reduced it to these three things. They are the first three things we ask ourselves about a man. We are absolutely brutal about this. If on the interviews and the tests a man lacks any one of these three things, he is scratched.

On helping people grow and develop

Query: What if a young manager does not believe in helping his people grow in stature and develop greater skill and competence?

Answer: We all know managers are dependent on their people for results, for the accomplishment of the group's or section's or department's mission. Will results be better or worse or just the same if the workers and managers the boss is responsible for are static, do things in a routine manner, are neither given nor themselves provide challenges, and do not grow in competence and stature?

We have concluded that no group is likely to be static, to stand still. Groups and the individuals composing them tend to improve or retrogress. Hence it is to the immediate and long-term interest of a boss to foster and assist the growth and development of the managers reporting to him.

For management development and performance measurement, a company, ATO, developed what it calls the "tag-along program" for middle managers. Harry E. Figgie, Jr. described the program as follows:

We've instituted what we call a "tag-along program" for middle management executives. One at a time we bring these fellows up and they stay in the corporate office with us and do everything we do. We've had them in acquisition discussions. We've had them in discussions for financing with the banks. These men in our middle management group tag along with the corporate management for one week. And believe me, they were all dragging at the end of that week. Too, at the end of the week we do something that we learned a long time ago and most managements hate to do. You know most managements appraise people. It's the toughest job of management. Our men are amazed to find out when we give them a Friday night evaluation, number one: that we know so much about what's going on in their division and their operation. And we make it very clear to them that if they're to progress, they have to go back and work on their weaknesses and we'll see them again in six months. That has quite a startling effect on some of these men. I've had them call me up and say, "I remember when you ate me out. I was going to call you and I decided no, I can handle this myself."

Figgie concluded, "It's really wonderful to watch these fellows grow."

To pursue further the idea of an individual manager's growth and development, let us consider Henry Luce. To us it is interesting that he started *Time* magazine with capital of $86,000 and by 1965 the value of the stock was $378 million; his personal ownership then amounted to $63 million. In writing about Luce in 1967, *Fortune* said:

He was perhaps the most attentive man of his time. His attention was not an outsized example of innate curiosity, prying at random; it was a carefully cultivated quality . . . first, the selective attention of a highly educated man, then the deepening and sharpening attention of a professional man.

Luce parlayed an inquiring mind into a fortune, and had a great impact on the United States. An inquiring mind is a great asset for a manager, young or old.

Thinking further about people and managing, we believe that the development of the people reporting to you is a specific responsibility each manager has and should discharge to the best of his/her ability. Yet it is our opinion that you cannot develop any man or woman who reports to you. We think management development—and, for that matter, individual development in any area of life for any adult—is basically a do-it-yourself job. We do believe, however, that you as a boss can set a climate that causes many of the people reporting to you to *want* to develop themselves. Your beliefs and attitudes, the way in which you delegate responsibility, your response to the first time one of your people makes a mistake, and many other things set a climate.

You may be familiar with McGregor's Theory X way of thinking about people as well as the Theory Y way, both of which were mentioned in Chapter 1. Theory X (oversimplified) says: People don't want to work; they're not trustworthy; you have to drive them. Theory Y claims people *do* want to work. Explain the task; give them guidelines or rules, then give them their heads. The results will please you. You may well have some theory of your own which is different from either of these. Whatever your basic ideas are about people, however, they will either help or hurt you in setting a climate for growth.

Another way to think about managing which relates both to your own development and that of your people is the Blake and Moulton Grid. Their managerial grid envisions a 9 x 9 checkboard grid. The vertical line concerns itself with people. Number 1 on this line indicates little concern and number 9 indicates great concern. The horizontal scale represents the degree of concern about production. Number 1 shows little concern for production and number 9 represents great concern.

A manager "ranked" as 6,3 would be evaluated as being 6/9ths of the way up the scale of concern for people, and 3/9ths of the way up the scale of concern for production. Some examples of evaluative rankings we would give to managers based on our analysis of Blake and Moulton's ideas are as follows:

1,1 is exemplified by a manager with no deep concern for either production (getting the work done) nor for people. In these days he is a marginal manager.

A 9,1 manager has a great concern about people. He wants them to find great satisfaction in their work. As a prototype, however, he exerts only enough effort on production to get by. In our opinion he should be more concerned about production.

A 1,9 manager is gung ho for getting the work out but regards the people as being there to perform a function to his satisfaction. He, as a prototype, has little concern about people as individuals. They are apt to be characterized by him as his "work force." This type of manager usually has people problems.

5,5 management strikes a balance between production and the personal satisfaction of the men and women in his unit. He is a "good" manager but far from the ultimate in "good" management.

A 9,9 manager achieves a great blend of superior production along with generally excellent morale. The men and women working for/with him know the production goals and are committed to making them, and usually do. These workers respect the boss and they feel they are members of a winning team. They find personal satisfaction in their work. This is the type of manager that young men and women in the early stages of their careers should seek to become, we believe.

If you haven't already thought in these terms, we suggest you may find it useful to do so. In Blake's and Moulton's terms where do you stand? Does that suit you, and your career goals? If not, do you want to change your status on the management grid? If so, it's a good idea to make a written step-by-step plan, with weekly or monthly checkups as to your progress.

On dealing persuasively with people

Query: What if a manager believes the best way to run things is just to tell the managers reporting to him what to do?

Answer: This suggests the manager sees little merit and may see great danger in a management style that does not abdicate but does share information and the reasons for proposed actions and uses persuasion and a selling approach most of the time as a management tool.

The authors have great faith in persuasion and selling as a management tool. We also believe in management by objectives, and in management by exception. They are all compatible.

Don't you know from personal experience that you like to be in the know? Don't you feel better if you know about company events and plans before you read about them in the newspaper? Don't you have more enthusiasm for a plan that you helped make or one that has been explained to you in detail as well as the ideas, events and reasoning behind the plan? Don't you like to be treated as a mature, interested, responsible businessman or -woman, and asked to express your views? Don't you work better if you know what the objectives are, and why they were settled on? Don't you like to be able to suggest objectives? Briefly, don't you like to be important and have your ego massaged?

If this can be done—in good faith—with sincerity—will the boss who does it be better off and the company too? Are the human resources in most businesses capable of doing better? If so, is consultative, participative management that uses people's ideas and is persuasive likely to pay off? The authors think it is.

The idea of consultative, participative management is good, but this should not obscure the fact that there are critical times when a boss needs to act in a way that is consonant with Theory X such as—"Let's don't discuss this, let's not argue about it—*you just go and do this right now.*"

In relation to a better utilization of human resources, meaning the people in his business, chairman Greenewalt, of DuPont, said something that you may find of interest and value:

It seems to me that the important qualifications that make for high competence in business leadership are intangible rather than tangible. They involve such things as the ability to deal with people sympathetically and understandingly, the ability to recognize competence in others, and the courage to weed out incompetence when necessary. They involve the ability to stimulate high performance at all organizational levels and to insure unity of purpose among individuals differing widely in temperament and experience.

Speaking of differing results secured by several companies, Greenewalt said:

The conclusion I have come to is that differences in managerial competence are due not to one person, nor to the few geniuses that cross the stage from time to time, but arise out of the creation of an atmosphere which induces every man or woman connected with the enterprise, no matter what their position, to perform his or her task with a degree of competence and enthusiasm measurably greater than what could be called their normal expectations.

Business success, then, can be measured by summing up the small increments of extra effort on the part of all the people who are joined together in a given enterprise. If one looks at the question quantitatively, it would seem inescapably that 5 percent or so extra performance on the part of, let us say, 90,000 people will far surpass extraordinary competence in a small executive group.

It is such modest differences in individual achievement, multiplied by many thousands, that distinguish a great company from one that is indifferent; and with equal truth, a great nation from its weaker neighbor.

Greenwalt, it seems to us, is saying, a favorable climate, resulting in plus performance, is better than having a few geniuses as top managers.

Query: How do you rate yourself as a climate-setter?

There are many reasons for creating a climate that is favorable for the growth and development of people reporting to you. The authors believe it is your responsibility to do this. They also believe it is a source of personal satisfaction to have helped others. In addition to assisting your people to grow and develop, it is worth noting that in some companies an individual can't be promoted unless he has working for him a good replacement. As a matter of fact, in building your own written career plan (which is discussed in Chapter 12) it is a good idea to include the training of a suitable successor. In some companies each manager is required to identify an individual who could succeed him today and also an individual who could succeed him in three years.

One reason some managers have for not helping people grow

and develop is that they are afraid their people will take their job. This fear is often an indication that the individual is a poor manager and may, among other things, lack self-confidence. It is a truism to say that if you don't believe in yourself it is unlikely anyone else will believe in you. Managers thrive when their people believe in them. Managers are in serious trouble when their people lack confidence in them. Self-confidence or lack of it is abundantly clear to the people who work for each individual manager. Among other things, there is a psychological reason for this that is embodied in the biblical quotation: "If the trumpet gives forth an uncertain sound, who will prepare himself for battle?" There is something in us that responds instinctively to a confident leader. Likewise, we have a negative reaction to a boss who is unsure of himself.

Do train, guide, help the growth and development of a potential successor and create a climate that makes all the managers reporting to you want to grow in stature and competence.

On setting high standards

Query: What if a manager says setting high standards is just pie in the sky? People will do what they have done. If high standards mean higher than now exist, then setting such high standards is a waste of time.

Answer: If people will just do what they have done, what is the necessity for and function of a manager? Is he to be a policeman to monitor the on-time and day-long presence of workers and/or managers? Is this enough to justify his existence and his pay? We think not. A group of clerical workers or of first-level managers are expected to perform better because they have a boss. If not, to raise the issue again, what are bosses for?

The authors would agree that raising standards is silly if a given group is performing at the top of its skill, all the work being done is necessary, and there can be no process changes or innovations. But the authors have rarely encountered or heard of such a situation.

Almost everyone who is likely to be working for you has his own desires and goals both economic and social. Also they have pride and skill. Aside from anyone who may have contracted the TGIF syndrome (Thank God It's Friday!), they are pleased with themselves when they work at or near the top of their skill. They know when they are performing at their top level. This gives them satisfaction. It is doubled when the boss gives them earned and deserved recognition and a sincere "well done." When this is the normal situation, they like the boss—the company—and their morale is high. When they also receive more money for superior performance, they are genuinely pleased.

If the boss also has created a climate of good will as well as the expectation of superior performance to meet high standards, then the individual is apt to be satisfied with or pleased with his fellow workers, in a social sense. It is the boss's job to see that his people are reasonably compatible—that they find personal (social) satisfaction within their group.

Low standards, sloppy operation, poor results, the feeling that others in the group are second-rate or slobs, is of little appeal, if not distasteful, to most of the people you'll manage. To the extent that the boss permits the above, the workers will come to work and say, "TGIF," and their morale will be low *because* most production workers, clerical workers, engineers and managers prefer the superior to the inferior, prefer to do their best rather than their worst, and prefer success to failure.

On rewarding superior performance and penalizing subpar performance

Query: What if a manager says rewarding superior performance and punishing poor performance doesn't apply here because all my people are about the same so far as results are concerned?

Answer: This suggests to the authors that the manager in question has evaluated his people and found only small differences in their performances, potential, and development. Such a situation has seldom been encountered by the authors, personally or second-hand. If and where such a situation is alleged to exist, we'd have to be convinced it is really so. For our present purpose, we elect to ignore such a situation, for to say the least it would appear to us to be exceedingly exceptional.

In talking about rewarding superior performance and penalizing subpar performance, it is obvious that one thing necessary is to have some way of appraising people's performance. The authors believe that in order to get a good, objective appraisal, it is necessary to write down what your conclusions are concerning essentials of the job. This suggests the need for a method. Many companies have a formal rating method. It often consists of two parts. One deals with factors affecting performance on the job, as well as a net conclusion as to how well the function has been performed. The other deals with the personal qualities and character of the individual being rated. If your company does not have a standard rating method, then you can make one of your own. In order to do this, list the various things you expect an individual to do and then decide as objectively as possible how well he has done his job. If development and character are important to you, spell out some appropriate details and objectively rate the employee on them.

If you create your own system, the rating can have as many graduations from "superior" to "poor" as you wish. One simple way to rate performance is to use "outstanding," "excellent," "good" and "fair." You will note that we have omitted listing "poor" as a rating. The reason for this is that our experience shows that very few managers will rate anyone as "poor." On the other hand, they seem to have no mental barriers to rating "fair" when in their judgment that is the proper rating. While we are not in favor of quantifying everything, you can if you wish assess a value of 4 to outstanding, 3 to excellent, 2 to good, and 1 to fair, and thereby cast up a numerical score. The higher the score, the better the individual's performance and personal qualities.

We believe that most of the people who work for you want to work and want to do a good job and will respond favorably to leadership that explains and inspires. As mentioned, we think high standards and high morale go together. Where there are high standards and high morale, employees feel they are on a winning ball club. The more they feel this way, the better the results. In other words, success feeds on success. The people who perform poorly should not be treated as well as the people who perform in a superior fashion. The subpar performance people should be moved in on and corrective measures should be taken. If the individual will respond, good. If, after an effort with enough time to reverse the trend there is no progress, then the individual who performs in a subpar fashion should be eliminated. Not to do so would leave a bad apple in the barrel that might contaminate some of the others.

In the authors' experience, people who work with other people know which ones are good and which ones aren't. They know who the producers are as well as those who drag their feet. But often they will not volunteer this information to the boss. One of the manager's jobs is to find out from the workers whose opinion he values who are the good producers and who are the poor ones. Frequent contact, rather than direct formal questioning, will enable the alert and sensitive manager to glean the opinion of one worker concerning one or more other workers. These views can be considered along with the manager's own objective conclusions and ratings.

People have to be convinced that the boss will promote them when they do a superior job and when there is an opportunity elsewhere in the business. When they see a boss doing this even though it hurts his own operation temporarily, the message comes through that he is on the level and will advance the interest of his superior people even when the cost to him is temporary trouble and inconvenience. When people see that the boss will not permit the good people he has trained to move into a better job but keeps them from his own purposes, then they know that the street they are on is a dead end. The result is that some quit trying to perform in a superior manner, or ask for a transfer.

If all the managers reporting to a boss are given the same base salary, the same pay increase, and the same bonuses, it is hard for the superior performers to believe that superior results are rewarded. In fact, when a manager claims that he will reward superior performance but doesn't do so, this becomes clear to most or all of his people. They then see the difference between what he says and what he does. The result is a credibility gap and a potentially useful managing tool is rendered ineffective.

Mutual dependence and individual independence

As Americans, we can say some things about the Pilgrims and
Plymouth Rock and the early Massachusetts Colony that bears
on the development of mutual dependence and individual
independence. First, the colonists were in favor of change,
improvement. They thought the circumstances and conditions of
their lives could be improved by leaving the Old World and going
to the New World. They were deeply discontented and greatly
hopeful. Second, the colonists produced the Mayflower Compact,
a simple declaration of moral law and acceptance of the Creator.
Third, in the early years faced with the dangers of an untamed
land and the ravages of disease and the threat of starvation, the
colonists worked together on the basis of "from each according
to his ability, to each according to his need." Farming was a
communal effort. The harvest went into a community storehouse
and was given out to individual families in accordance with their
needs as decided on by Governor Bradford. There was a clear
recognition of mutual dependence.

Did this work out well? No, it did not. So, after several years
of near disaster Governor Bradford decided to change the
scheme of things. Fourth, Governor Bradford decreed, with the
consent of the governed, that in the future each man would
plant what he pleased when he pleased and any resulting harvest
would belong to him. Clearly the idea was that he who grew the
most and whose hunting was most successful could eat well.
Equally clearly, he who grew little and hunted with small success
would not eat well.

Did this work? It did. In his diary, Governor Bradford wrote:
"It was noticed that not only men but also women and children
labored in the fields." Also he noted, "From that year on
neither famine nor hunger afflicted the colony."

Thus in the Massachusetts Colony mutual dependence with no
reward for superior performance failed, while individual independence prospered. While true, such a simplistic conclusion is
to misread truth. Complete dependence on the group effort
failed. Continued dependence on the members of the group and
its leaders for spiritual aid and comfort, the preservation of law,

order and protection against the common enemy worked. Specific individual rewards for specific individual effort and achievement worked.

This was a "mixed" economy and political and social order— mutual dependence in areas where this was appropriate and worked, with individual independence in first economic affairs and later in other realms.

The lesson of our early history, as well as the intervening years and of the present moment is that Americans more than most other peoples have recognized the wisdom of combining group effort and group strength and group unity (mutual dependence) with the best efforts of individuals stimulated by their pride, their competitive instinct, and the freedom to keep what they produced as modified by taxes which are believed to be generally just and required by the needs of society.

Now, back to managing. Managing in a corporate situation or a small partnership or individual proprietorship is devoted to:

1. Combining the skills of several up to hundreds of thousands of people, so that—
2. There is a lot of output per individual, so that—
3. A worthwhile service or product is produced, so that—
4. A profit (necessary to pay individuals whose savings financed the business a reward and to buy tools needed for future production) is earned.

This is a voluntary association of people. It is successful to the degree that genuine and lasting cooperation exists and is practiced.

A note worthy of mention is that starting in Colonial days men and women gave up some of their independence as an individual shoemaker (cobbler) or housewife (seamstress) to go into a factory because:

1. They could earn a higher wage and/or—
2. Work fewer hours for the same wage and/or—
3. They were relieved of the necessity for decision making.

The workers needed a boss to deal with such things as what to make—in what kinds of grades and styles—how much to make

—how sizable an inventory to build, if any—who would provide the money to buy raw materials and pay the workers and carry the accounts receivables. Bosses were needed. They performed an essential function.

Managers today don't just manage machines or cash or research. They manage people who run machines, people who loan money, and people who do research. So one thing a young manager should be very clear on is—does he like people? Does he like to be with people?

Query: What would be your preference if you had to choose between two positions: (1) a head waiter in a busy restaurant; (2) the lone keeper of a lighthouse?

Answer: Clearly the head waiter will be an unhappy man and likely unsuccessful if he dislikes people, doesn't want to be with people, and regards dealing with people as a cross he has to bear. Equally clearly, a man who likes people, wants to be with people, and dislikes isolation will hardly find the position of a lone lighthouse keeper interesting and compatible. In fact, he is likely to be frustrated and miserable.

So we are back to the matter of your basic beliefs and attitudes discussed in Chapter 1 and which play a large part in the success or failure of a manager.

Some conclusions

The authors offer for your consideration ten conclusions. They are:

Conclusion 1: Successful managers like rather than dislike people.

Conclusion 2: Successful managers have the ability to select a specific individual who can and will perform well in a specific job.

Conclusion 3: Successful managers have the skill to select a specific individual who can and will perform well in a specific job *and* has the potential for further growth, development, and promotion to a position of greater responsibility. Conclusion 3 is based on the belief that almost all business could use to advantage more promotable people than they now possess. The authors can recall only one business that encountered serious personnel problems because it had at one time more promotable people than it had places for them.

Conclusion 4: Though people are important and output is important, full satisfaction to people at the cost of output or maximum output accompanied by serious dissatisfaction of people should not be accounted satisfactory. A manager must possess and exercise balance. A motor won't function with no gasoline even though it has plenty of oil. A full tank and no oil for the motor doesn't produce long-term performance. We need both gas and oil. A manager needs both a real interest in and concern for people, and a real interest in and concern for production.

Conclusion 5: A boss with a secretary depends on her. A secretary depends on her boss. A man or woman hired by a manager depends on him. A manager who hires a man or woman depends on them. A manager can't make it alone. He needs help from his people *and* his boss.

Conclusion 6: If you would achieve extraordinary success, get your people to carry a torch for you. Get your people, your boss, and others to cheer for you, carry a torch for you, because you are super good with people, because you and your people achieve superior results, and because you are not only a fine manager and boss but a fine guy or gal. As to the last, we don't mean merely popular or well-liked, but we do mean well-respected, well-regarded as a man or woman of outstanding merit and worth. We do mean a man or woman of good character who acts in accordance with principle and is not swayed by fear or greed. We do not mean a so-called perfect man or woman, for we all have human frailties, but we do mean what they meant in the Old West when they said, "He'll do to ride the river with." In brief, we mean a man or woman to be respected, trusted, and even admired. The kind of man or woman most parents hope their children will become.

It's harder to succeed if your people don't help you a lot. It's still harder and almost impossible to succeed if your people are against you. It's easier to succeed if people, your boss, your associates, your people, are enthusiastically for you. They will be if:

Conclusion 7:
You use your common sense and good judgment.
You are generally fair.
You are reasonably consistent.
You believe in your people.
You help your people grow.
You defend your people when they need it and you can do so in good conscience.
You show your respect and esteem for your people by helping them grow in self-confidence and by treating them as individuals of dignity, merit and worth.

Conclusion 8: Have the guts to punish failure and to adequately reward success. The two following conclusions, though not related to matters discussed in this chapter are, the authors believe, both valid and self-evident.

Conclusion 9: Know your business, its objectives, purposes, processes, methods, if you want to be a successful manager.

Conclusion 10: Know enough about competitors so that you are a vigorous and ethical competitor yourself. (Knowledge of your business and your industry and the external environment which embraces many things including your competitors is the subject of the next chapter.)

The following observations on people came from 13 practical operating managers.

Helping my people to grow and develop (one manager's ideas)

I can best summarize my ideas and actions on this by saying that I encourage each person to learn not only his or her own specific area of responsibilities, but learn about other areas of our store or stores. I consider it one of my prime responsibilities (other than to make a profit) to help people grow and develop in our company, for their personal satisfaction and gain and for the future growth of the company. I do encourage my subordinates to aim for the long term, not just immediate gains, and try very hard to help them in these aims. This involves their basic daily tasks, helping them on long-term planning, conducting special training meetings or having them conduct these meetings, keeping them informed as often as possible, letting them know not only their goals but asking them to establish their own goals, giving them standards of performance and requiring these standards to be met (as near as possible), and salary rewards as deserved are given—formal reviews twice each year with informal reviews as often as needed.

This is how I see my role; they may see it in a different light. My first requirement is for mutual respect—liking them or being liked is secondary, although desirable.

From a purely selfish part for *myself* as well as the *company*, the stronger my subordinates, the stronger my own individual performance and the results expected.

Helping my people to grow and develop (a second manager's ideas)

Several of the people in my prior job (mostly in the supervisory categories) were around 55-60 years of age, and most had been in the same department and essentially the same job for 20-25 years. When I first went into this position, I recognized that quite frankly, my success or failure was dependent on these three or four people, as I had no prior experience in this field. At the same time, I had developed good relations with these men during the term I was in our corporate accounting, and to a great degree I used my past experience to acquaint them, on a day-to-day basis with how their work fit into the "big picture," and why it was important to do things a certain way. With this approach, I was able to develop some "quick respect" from these people, and also the people they were supervising. Ultimately, I was able to initiate changes that were normally accepted by them (some weren't worth a damn) and, overall, I would say that in the short time I was there (a little over a year), beneficial changes were made (some of which they started suggesting), and relations with other departments improved greatly by these three or four people's change in attitude.

Helping my people to grow and develop (a third manager's ideas)

I do the following:

1. Take advantage of company training programs.

2. Delegate authority and responsibility and glory. I rarely ever speak for these people to higher management levels. Each person gets to explain his own portion of overall agreed to plan.

I rarely ever listen to a problem that is not accompanied by recommended solution. If the solution is not applicable (possible) for outside reasons, I try to be sure that these reasons are explained fully.

If financial opportunities are identified and cannot be acted on, the reason is relayed quickly to the person who identified the opportunity.

I insist that "team" recommendations and/or conflicts are exposed and known before recommendation presentations are made.

Helping my people to grow and develop (a fourth manager's ideas)

1. I allow them to establish their own "priority projects" over and above basic job responsibilities—getting mutual agreement on them and allowing them to do their own self-evaluation against measured results expected.

2. I get mutual agreement of identified needs; for example, experience, know-how, accountability, and agreeing to a development program designed to meet those needs.

3. I lead weekly discussions of problems, opportunities, and possible changed course of actions.

Helping my people to grow and develop (a fifth manager's ideas)

1. Routine counseling (formal and extemporaneous).

2. Promote exposure to key executive personnel.

3. Promote cross-training for marketability, broadened interests, increased understanding of the bigger picture, realistic goal setting.

4. Delegation of primary responsibility for project budgets, salary budgets, and merit salary awards, employee morale and loyalty.

5. Deliberate and continuing communication of company objectives and goals.

6. Provide direct assistance in sorting out and setting of personal and project objectives and goals including priorities and timing. Re-evaluation of these on an informal and formal basis.

7. Timely recognition of accomplishments; both positive and negative accomplishments.

8. Promote a reasonably free and open (direct) line of communication at all levels. This includes both business and social environments.

9. Try to understand personal problems and be reasonably accomodative.

10. Always maintain a positive, urgent, aggressive, sincere action/reaction at all levels of personnel interaction.

11. Maintain a consistency of image, words and actions.

12. Recognize and reward on the basis of technical/administrative accomplishments and potential.

Helping my people to grow and develop (a sixth manager's ideas)

1. Create an environment which allows subordinates to manage their own operation.

2. Permit free exchange of ideas and constructive conflict in meetings.

3. Establish, with the managers, goals and objectives.

4. Utilize company training courses.

5. Hold managers responsible for meeting objectives.

6. Be a good listener.

7. Have subordinates represent me to my superiors.

8. Solicit ideas and criticisms from subordinates.

9. If in error, admit my mistakes.

10. Set a good example of appearance and conduct.

11. Periodically review operations of subordinates and have critical review of same.

12. Conduct formal personnel evaluation at least yearly, informal ones on an ongoing basis.

13. Have a subordinate "sit in my chair" when I am absent.

14. Have a basic trust in the willingness of my subordinates to want to do the best job they can.

People, commitment, and communications
(a seventh manager's ideas)

1. I feel that I have the ability to get along well with my superiors, peers, and subordinates, in carrying out my job duties.

2. I feel that I am committed to my job and the company (goals) and try to convey this to the people working for me.

3. I encourage good communications within my department and welcome and listen carefully to all feedback from my personnel.

4. I respect the opinions of other people and while I might not always agree, I state my objections!

5. I feel that I am fair in my dealings with other people.

People
(an eighth manager's ideas)

I think the manager who treats his people as his first priority is on the right track. He should keep in close, "interested" touch with all the key people. Further, he should use the subtle means of suggestions and reinforcement whenever possible rather than commands (you ought to do this or that or else, etc.). Your key people probably respond better to subtle rather than blunt directives.

People getting credit
(a ninth manager's ideas)

It used to "bug" me to work on important projects, submit them to my boss, and have them submitted to corporate head-quarters under his name. Later I found myself doing the same thing, after making revisions for what I judged poor quality. In talking this over with my staff, I found that some thought "Why should I try to be perfect, when you're going to make changes anyway?" Now, we both sign. This has resulted in the preparer doing a much better job because he knows he will get credit for the report, while my signature indicates that I'm still accepting responsibility.

People
(a tenth manager's ideas)

The president of my division has what I consider to be a management technique that has always impressed me greatly. While it is probably not unique, it is accomplished only by a deliberate effort. Bill knows each of the approximately 300 employees in our division by their full name and in almost all cases, the name and occupation of their spouse as well. This is an accomplishment that is noted by each of these employees.

People
(an eleventh manager's ideas)

The greatest single responsibility which a manager has, in my opinion, is the taking of the time to express his *sincere* interest in his people and then devoting his time and effort toward *earning the right* to justify their respect and complete confidence.

Over the past several years I have utilized a plan which I termed *face-to-face.* This plan works, briefly, as follows:

1. All of the people with whom I have a direct working relationship have their names entered into a notebook which I keep in my sole possession.

2. Depending upon the needs as we mutually see them, I visit *privately* with each of these people not less than twice each year. The visit is done at a time when there will be no interruption. For example, if in the office, the visit can take place early or late in the day. There is no time limit and each visit takes from one and a half to two hours.

3. After a mutual understanding of the term "career goals" we proceed to learn what commitments each of us must make in order to enable the employee to accomplish his goals, and prepare myself to be as well-qualified as possible to aid him in the pursuit of these goals.

After a mutual respect and confidence is *begun,* the frequency of the need to have these *face-to-face* visits becomes apparent to both of us. There are certain guidelines which I must follow to insure continuing success with this kind of effort:

1. Be always *available* (fully and complete) through use of an "open door" policy.
2. Be *honest.* (You may not always like what you hear but you'll be able to respect that you have no doubts as to where you stand.)
3. Be *fair* (but firm when necessary).
4. Be always mindful of the urgent necessity to be *sincere.*
5. Be a *good listener.*

It follows, then, that there are many resultant benefits to the employee, the company, and to self; some of which are (1) the employee always knows where he stands and what is expected from him; (2) he knows, therefore, what he has the right to expect; (3) the company has a manager who is well-qualified to guide the careers of his top people; and I benefit greatly from making a significant contribution to others.

People, economics, theory
(a twelfth manager's ideas)

I tend to separate management into three areas, appreciating that they are related. I will address these as, "people," "economic," and "theory."

The "people" area appears to me to be the only asset which I as a general manager can directly influence and control. All end results are primarily due to the technical efforts of other people. I must accomplish my goals through these others. My experience as a manager is that I must train, tantalize, test, and trust my people. I must train them in what must be done, how to accomplish the goals, and how to evaluate the results. I must tantalize them with the desire to contribute and the self-satisfaction derived from a job well done. I must continually test the results of my efforts against the goals I have set. I must trust my people to accept the challenge and accomplish the desired results, and I must trust myself to accept the results accomplished by others as an extension of myself.

Although people are my major resource as a manager, I must also be constantly alert to other resources. Time is a major resource which I must make the best use of and help other people do likewise. Other "economic" areas are money, raw materials, and energy. Adequate accounting and control for these items must be established. Particularly energy (both thermo-dynamic and human) must be conserved and diverted to the most effective uses.

"Theory" I define as how "people" and "economics" are properly utilized. I find that management by objectives is an effective management tool. This requires a thorough understanding of the roles of both the employee and supervisor. As a supervisor I have the people prepare a list of 20 items which defines what their job is. Independently I do the same. We then sit down and compare lists. From this we understand what each expects of the other. I do this yearly. After we agree as to what the job is, we then prepare objectives for the individual—again independently—then combined. We jointly review this list quarterly and update to current needs. This assumes frequent one-on-one communications and keeps our goals and progress in front of us.

Choosing and training a successor
(a thirteenth manager's ideas)

Many managers seem so bound up in their work that they fail to see the need to install and train others to take their place. Indeed many see it as a threat to their security. Some, being pushed into the situation, appoint two assistants who can then "fight each other and not me." I do not believe in this negative approach as it has a bad effect on the necessary harmony of a division or department.

Choice of a successor is always difficult. To appoint a real doer with a light of battle in his eyes, knowing that his eventual succession and success might make one's own efforts as division or department head seem mediocre in comparison, poses a problem to some managers. However, a manager with self-confidence who believes he will be promoted will pick as his successor a man or woman of ability and promise. A growing company has opportunities for everyone.

On the two occasions when I have been in the fortunate position of asking for and getting a possible successor I have found the following ground rules useful:

1. Don't necessarily look for someone who would be a second "you."

2. Don't tell him at the time of his joining the department he's a possible successor, simply let him be accepted as another member of the department. Then both he and you can evaluate the situation; you in such a situation have the knowledge of foresight. It also means that if he doesn't make the grade, he doesn't feel put down. Of course, this particular criteria may not apply if he applies for and is accepted for such a position beforehand rather than as part of an internal move.

3. Watch in particular his effect on and manner with those whom he will eventually control. Their assessment of him will soon be apparent.

4. To train, try to delegate some work from the start, realizing of course that unless he's already a member of the division, it will take a couple of weeks to reorientate. If he's entirely new, insure that an introductory program is set up to allow him to meet those he will be communicating with in other divisions and also get a visual picture of the overall structure and facilities of the company. Let him sit in at meetings with you at the earliest opportunity (once you've decided that he will succeed you). Discuss the agenda before the meeting and let him contribute to the makeup of your information for such a meeting. It will be here that he will first get to know the personalities and their foibles.

We believe a great conceptualizer who is a profound thinker and very people sensitive has little chance of achieving success as a manager in a business enterprise if he doesn't know a good deal about his business and industry.

The higher one moves in the management ranks, the more vital is knowledge of the external environment. If chief executive officers' compensation was given in components, I think the ability to predict the future in social, economic, and political terms with a 75 percent batting average on matters of significance to his business should account for 50 percent of his pay.

Paul M. Hammaker

Skilled or professional managers cannot usually manage businesses where they have had no prior experience. They could only do so if they were given two or three years to learn it, and this the world won't give.

Louis T. Rader

4

*Managing principle
number two: Understand
what you are managing
through a knowledge of
your business, industry,
and environment*

Because businesses are not all alike, it is important for young
managers to become well-informed early in their careers about
their specific business and industry. There is a great deal of
empirical know-how contained in every business. Some of it is
referred to as industry practice, some as custom, some as tradi-
tion. Most of it has never been reduced to writing. The magnitude and complexity of this know-how was only appreciated
when industries started to develop management systems utilizing
computers. The fantastic cost in time and money spent in trying
to codify and manage going operations has literally put some
businesses into bankruptcy. Those that succeeded got a new
awareness of how hard it was to reduce every procedure and
every decision-making process to a computer software program.
Many still don't appreciate this fact and so have distorted
management training by neglecting one of its most important
aspects—namely, that what is to be managed, its qualities,
characteristics and fundamentals must be taken into account in
trying to apply the principles of management.

The theory that a well-trained manager could be equally
successful in any kind of business has been promoted by many
advocates of professional management. This theory held that

there were principles of management which, if learned, enabled the manager to guide and direct any business. This theory does violence to the fact that business and industries are significantly different. Just as it is known that to successfully operate in a foreign country a person should understand the language, the idiom, the values, and the culture of the country, so a business-man should understand, or be aware of, the historical back-ground, and the specific characteristics of the business he is in. These characteristics may take many forms, such as buying habits of customers, leasing, handling of receivables, discount structures, extent of R&D expenditures, union strength in the industry, progress payments, and so on.

There is no question but that many business financial measurements and controls can be, and are, very similar. However, the significance of the numbers is different for different businesses as is pointed out in Chapter 7. An average of 60 days to 90 days receivable may be normal for one business and catastrophic for another. Why this may be so depends on the kind of industry involved.

The management principles usually covered in textbooks and executive training courses are under the major headings of planning, organizing, staffing, measurements, climate, control, and leadership, many of which are covered in part in this text. The authors believe, however, that management principles are of little real use unless they are studied in the context of the business or industry they are being applied to.

Not to realize this is as though aircraft pilots training were carried out entirely from textbooks, operating procedures, and in simulators, without reference to the characteristics of the plane to be flown. Or to train men to get them into good physical condition and then to expect them to excel equally in any sport, whether it be tennis, basketball, or golf.

A manager can manage anything?

The higher one gets in the management hierarchy, the more nearly may the above phrase be true. There are many examples of men who have gone, for example, from a law firm which handled a company's affairs to president of that company. Such moves are often in response to major environmental forces which the company finds itself in, and the board of directors responds to that need by hiring someone who is strong in the required area. There are certain major risks in this procedure, but we are not concerned with them here since we are addressing ourselves to the younger person who is still in a functional spot. For one who operates at this functional level—say one who directs engineering, marketing, manufacturing, merchandising, purchasing, or finance, or one subset of each of these—we believe that it is almost impossible to be successful without real specific knowledge of the functional areas. Otherwise, how can he appraise the capability of his people and organization? How can he guide the developments or appraise creativity? How can a manager teach or constructively criticize? How can he adequately represent or defend his organizational objectives, or performance, with other functional managers in the inevitable and necessary arguments which occur in meetings where best solutions are sought? How can he be sure that his own component's estimate on projects in time or money are realistic or reasonable? Or even whether a story he gets makes sense?

The answers to these and many other questions has to be that he cannot accomplish these necessary functions of his job with just a theory of management, no matter how good that theory may be. Given a highly intelligent and motivated man, he can learn fast, but a year or two is easily lost—a year or two in which the leader is trying to catch up to his organization. Few companies can or should want such a situation.

This particular distortion is found more frequently in big companies than in smaller ones, perhaps because more "professional managers" are found in bigger companies. Small companies' executives are closer to their business, or maybe they just have or apply more common sense. If they need a bricklayer, they find out whether the man they are talking to has laid bricks; a truck driver, whether he has driven a truck; teacher, whether he has taught. The "professional manager" who has a liberal education background often has too little understanding of the intricacies and complexity of a functional area and, accordingly, has often completely misjudged the importance of the technology or the marketing approach or the financial decisions.

The most extreme case we know of, occurred in a big company, then in the computer business. Three executives in series, a general manager, division manager, and group executive, were satisfied to pick as manager of engineering, an extremely brilliant and personable man who had not worked with computers, had never designed one, nor worked in a component that did. The man worked as hard as he could, did learn a lot very rapidly, but was not able to make any contribution to the business the first year, and was relieved of his job within two years. The complete unwillingness of the management to recognize the special nature of computer engineering was unfair to company and man alike. It is no wonder they were not very successful.

In this case they could not appreciate the fact that a person successful as a manager in one kind of engineering would not automatically be equally successful in another radically different one. The higher the technology, the greater the odds are that he will be unsuccessful.

Ignorance is not bliss

There are at least two degrees of ignorance. One is to not know, and the other is to not know that you don't know. The second state is much worse than the first and to stay out of it one must look around.

Management may be in part an art, but knowledge of a business must be real. Leadership style may be important, but knowledge of the business is at least equally important. Management by objectives is good, but the objectives had better be based on a sound knowledge of the fundamentals of the manager's particular business.

People who move into new jobs, or different jobs, or from school into a job are usually aware of the fact that they don't know much about the new job. However, they often don't realize the importance of learning about it, and the importance of learning fast. Nor do they consciously know how to attack the problem.

There are some fundamentals which can be stated as usually true. One is that people working in the component, who have been there a while, do know a great deal about the business. A second is that most people want to help a new employee unless he turns them off by being too aggressive, or arrogant, or objectionable in some other way, or because they see him as a threat. A third is that each working area of a component has certain characteristics and variables.

A realization that these characteristics exist in any new job is a first step toward the necessary know-how. A young person in a new job should then identify the subject areas he intends to learn about—identify the most important and schedule his learning.

For one thing, he cannot or should not make any suggestions unless he knows what he is talking about. Even questions to those around him should demonstrate some understanding of the environment. Perhaps the worst kind of question to ask a principal of a firm is, "Why are we in this business"? After the surprised stare, or "Say that again" response, the answer is likely to be, "For the same reason anybody is in any business." But more important, some damage has been done to the young man, for although he may have thought it to be a very provocative, deep question, his boss's reaction is probably less than complimentary to him. Yet most knowledge of a specific situation must come from asking questions or, at least, discussions with individuals in that area.

The learning process should be broken into pieces: First, specific knowledge of the component of the business in which the man is working and its interrelations with the overall division or company; second, specific knowledge of the larger unit of which that component is a part; third, specific knowledge of the entire company.

We believe strongly that it helps to write down such findings, particularly in the first six months on the job. If written, a young new employee can, for instance, approach his boss and say, "I have written down what I think are the major characteristics of operating principles of this component (unit, section, department). I wonder if you would tell me whether I have it straight as far as you are concerned." The chances are good that the boss has never written them down and would be quite interested not only in evaluating the write-up but adding to it.

Toward an understanding

Another starting point for the young manager to establish know-how about his business is to ask himself certain questions. If he is in manufacturing: "What are the *significant* differences of this business from others?" Some starting points would be to develop investment per production worker and investment per total employee. This kind of data is readily available from the Conference Board reports or even from some business magazine publications. It will be found that there is over a ten to one range for this number in U.S. industry.

A following question could be: "What is the direct labor content as a percent of sales?" Again there is over a ten to one range. Is it of value to know that your industry has a high or low labor content? We think so. Then, numbers should be developed for costs as a percentage of sales by functional areas, R&D engineering, marketing, finance. We have heard many managers say, "Our business is capital intensive," and when they are asked, "What do you mean? What is the number that tells you it is? Where does it stand in this respect to other industries?" They often don't know. They should, though, and young managers who do know place themselves in a favorable situation. And similarly with the phrase "labor intensive." At what point can it be said that a business is labor intensive? When labor is 10 percent, or 20 percent, or 40 percent of the sales dollar?

The next kind of question to be asked to gain an understanding of the business is, "So what?" What difference does it make if my business is labor intensive or is not labor intensive? The very asking of this question can start to promote understanding of the fundamentals of the business. If labor is not a very significant element of cost, what are the significant ones? And how should this affect short- and long-range planning in product, plant, and people? Does it mean that emphasis must be on creative design and automation rather than skill in manufacturing? Does it mean the company has a good opportunity to carry its expertise overseas, or the opposite?

A different kind of question must be asked in the service industries. Whereas all manufacturing business can be rank-ordered in investment per worker, or output per square foot, because they are all involved in producing a physical output, the service industries do not admit of these same generalizations. It is not meaningful to compare hospital performance to retail stores, or to railroads, or to telephone companies. But within any one service category, significant numbers can be looked for in order to identify specific characteristics, or even idiosyncrasies of the business. Learning and knowing significant numbers is a first step toward understanding the nature of the business and what influences its success. Later, as a young manager gains experience and progresses, he needs to become familiar with interrelationships over some period of time so that a great deal of the data becomes the background for his intuitions, or gut feelings. Researchers in the field of computers have concluded that there are certain aspects of human thought which are essential for managerial decision making. These include "fringe consciousness," defined as an awareness of cues in the environment which are too numerous to be considered explicitly; "ambiguity tolerance," a willingness to deal with variables that are not precisely defined, but are useful to the problems at hand, and "essence"—the ability to sort out the necessary from the incidental characteristics. It is our feeling that all these aspects come from extensive and intensive participation in and study of the business—which should be achieved by the time one has progressed into the higher ranks of middle management.

In the middle and higher executive ranks of a company, great interest in, concern for, and knowledge of the external environment is necessary. In the world beyond the walls of a factory, or sales office or store or bank lie the company's customers; competitors' customers; the product line or services of competitors; company suppliers of materials, parts, and services; the work force of all types from unskilled labor through executives· unions; sources of money and credit; professional services covering accounting, law, management consultants, and many

FIGURE 1
THE EXTERNAL ENVIRONMENT

The external environment is characterized by change and uncertainty.
The General Manager needs to appraise and evaluate key factors such as:

Competition	Unions
Customers	Workers
Suppliers	Accountants
Sources of money	Lawyers
Sources of credit	Consultants

State of technology
State of the economy
Pressure groups
Government laws and
   regulations

The General Manager needs to identify opportunities and dangers,
determine resources needed to "cash in" on opportunities and to
combat dangers (are the required resources available?), decide
probability of success, determine "reward" if success is achieved, and
spell out in detail the "penalty" if opportunity is acted upon and the
plan *fails*.

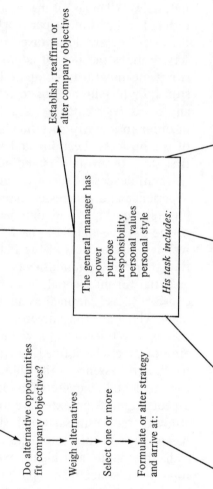

Do alternative opportunities
fit company objectives?

→ Weigh alternatives

→ Select one or more

→ Formulate or alter strategy
   and arrive at:

The general manager has
   power
   purpose
   responsibility
   personal values
   personal style

   His task includes:

Establish, reaffirm or
alter company objectives

The strategy to be implemented

Strategy formulation includes:

Inventory, evaluate, and "understand" company resources;

Establish, reaffirm or alter company objectives so that they make sense related to internal resources, external environment, the GM's purpose, the GM's responsibility, the GM's personal values;

Determine in the changing external environment opportunities and dangers;

Determine available "alternative" courses of action; they can be offensive (grow) or defensive (protect) or both;

Test alternatives versus company objectives, resources, and the GM's purpose, responsibility, and personal values;

Choose among alternatives the ones that best fit the company, including degree of risk, amount and kind of resources required, probability of success, reward for success, and penalty for failure;

Formulate new strategy (it may be the existing one, modified or expanded);

Then, if necessary, alter the existing structure in appropriate ways so the new strategy can be put into effect.

Nature of general management

Integrative

Ultimate responsibility

Time: Sequence / Span

Timing: Does longer-range planning than do the functional managers; manages so customers are created and/or satisfied; encourages, secures innovative thinking and action.

Inventory and evaluate

The form

The location and size of resources on hand or availability of:

Executive manpower
Sales force
Distribution network
Technical manpower
Office and clerical people
Production workers
Service organization
Good union relations
Know-how
Distinctive competences
Technological superiority
Plant, machinery, equipment
Reputation
Patents
Money

Relating

"Relating" is a key word in the general manager's life and job. In fact, you could almost describe his job as one of understanding relationships and arriving at new, practical relationships that promise improved results. For example, to be a strategy maker and a structure builder, he has to relate:

Resources to opportunities
Opportunities to risk
Organization structure to chosen strategy
Strategy to objectives
Performance to budgets
Cash needs to cash resources
Rewards to superior performance
Penalties to failures
Products or services to markets
Market plans to competition
His pre-planned response to probable changes in competitor's marketing programs
Profitability to market share
Information system to decision making
Personal qualifications of individuals to meet job requirements
Risk of acting to risk of inaction

Structure

Building or altering structure so it is appropriate and effective in implementing the chosen strategy.

Task definition
Task assignment
Task acceptance
Decision-making/where located?
Reporting relationships
Organizational climate and behavior and style wanted
Hiring, training, promotion, firing managers
Standards
Planning
Budgeting
Control techniques
Reporting system
Performance measurement of activities and managers
Reward
Punishment

specialized services such as tax guidance and labor relations assistance; public pressure groups; government laws and regulations; the state of technology; the state of the economy; and the general public.

Any young man who aspires to high business positions will find it to his advantage to become increasingly knowledgeable about external affairs, conditions, and trends.

In our teaching directed to practicing middle management and senior executives, as well as to aspiring graduate school students, we emphasize the importance of knowing well the factors external to a business that are so important now and are steadily becoming more important, as well as the key internal elements. We use Figure 1—with the general manager in the middle of things—to show one way to look at his multifaceted responsibilities. Figure 1 gives a quick bird's-eye view of the tasks of the general manager and senior executives. Also some of our businessmen students and our MBAs who plan to go into business have used this general scheme in their own career planning. They put themselves in the center and consider their objectives, resources, and opportunities, and create a career strategy plan.

How can a young manager gain knowledge of his area, his company, and his industry?

In his own job the young manager has known responsibility and produces and/or receives reports dealing with important facets of his operation. Beyond this he will likely feel a need for some more information. If he does, he should dig it out and use it. If he can't do this, he should request the information (or assistance in getting it from his boss if necessary) from the accounting department or the industrial engineer or the advertising manager or whoever has the needed information, knowledge, and expertise.

In publicly-owned companies he can get and read the company's proxy statement and annual report. He also will receive or can request all information available to employees and the public. In relation to industry knowledge, he should read the leading trade publications.

Probably a young manager will have no difficulty identifying and securing the appropriate trade publications. If this is not the case, the N. W. Ayer *Directory of Newspapers and Periodicals* has more than 100 pages of trade publication lists ranging from advertising and marketing, automatic control systems, autos and aviation through metal working and metal trade and ending with such listings as refrigeration and warehousing. A further source of information is *National Organizations of the United States,* published by Gale Research Company, Detroit. It has over 250 pages of trade, business, and commercial organizations. Many of them maintain libraries, conduct research, hold conferences, compile statistics and offer other types of services such as educational campaigns and courses.

For many areas of U.S. business, short courses are offered— for example, by the American Management Association, as mentioned earlier. Industry groups such as the American Institute of Banking and many universities and colleges also offer short courses. The young manager interested in learning more should ask to be sent to such a course when he believes it appropriate.

In addition to reading trade journals, technical material, and other information dealing with the industry, the young manager is well-advised, we believe to read general publications such as *The Wall Street Journal, Fortune, Business Week, Forbes, U.S. News and World Report.* Many young managers decide to discover what their boss reads—in both the specialized and general fields. Then they do the same. The purpose being to understand their boss and his thinking better.

Of course, reading is an adjunct to business-time, and since time is not unlimited every young manager has to work out his own time allotment for reading as well as set his priorities so that he gets a maximum return for the time he invests in reading and study.

Finally, there are some books outside of a manager's special field that are worth reading such as Peter Drucker's *The Effective Executive* and others shown on the following list.

Recommended reading. The following are references to books on business and management, which the authors have found to be very useful. We believe that a book becomes valuable when it is first studied, and then used as a reference when advice or help is sought. A single casual reading will probably not make a purchase worthwhile.

The Golden Book of Management
Edited for the International Committee of Scientific Management (CIOS) by L. F. Urwick, Newman Neame, Ltd., London, 1956.

Col. L. F. Urwick, a noted British author and management consultant, was commissioned by the International Committee of Scientific Management to bring together in one volume a short biography of those persons who in the opinion of the International Committee have made original and outstanding contributions to the world body of knowledge about the subjects of management and/or administration. It does not contain the name of any person still living. You will be interested to find among Americans listed, names like Filene and McKinsey. Col. Urwick has also written an excellent discussion on considerations governing the number of people who can report to a manager.

The Functions of the Executive
Chester I. Barnard, Harvard University Press, 1938.

By any measurement this book is a real classic of the management field. Barnard at the time he wrote this book was president of the N.J. Bell Telephone Company. He had worked his way up from a starting job as lineman. Though the book is excellent, the style is such that it is very hard to read, somewhat akin to reading Milton's poems.

Dynamic Administration
The Collected Papers of Mary Parker Follett, edited by Metcalf and Urwick, Harper & Bros., 1940.

M. P. Follett, born in Boston in 1869, wrote some truly remarkable papers on organization, constructive conflict, and the giving of orders. Her concept of "The Law of the Situation" (p. 58 ff.) has been, and still is, of great value.

The Evaluation Interview
Richard A. Fear, McGraw-Hill (2d ed., 1973).

Richard Fear was vice president of the Psychological Corp. in New York City. His book is much more than a guide for interviewing, important as that is. It is really a book on applied psychology put together from information learned and collated over several thousand interviews of middle and top managers.

The Human Side of Enterprise
Douglas McGregor, McGraw-Hill, 1960.

This is the excellent, easy-to-read book which develops the Theory X and Theory Y views. It also has many good references for those interested in social science knowledge about human nature and behavior.

Self-Renewal: The Individual and the Innovative Society
John W. Gardner, Harper & Row, 1963.

John Gardner has been Secretary of HEW, president of the Carnegie Corporation, and a professor of psychology. Currently he is the head and moving spirit of Common Cause. He is the author of several books and in addition he has written some wonderful papers such as, "We, The People," "The Anti-Leadership Vaccine," "How to Prevent Organizational Dry Rot."

Career Management
Marion S. Kellogg, American Management Assoc., Inc., 1972.

Miss Kellogg is the author of several books, among them, *What to Do about Performance Appraisal; Closing the Performance Gap; Putting Management Theories to Work,* and *When Man and Manager Talk.* She was once a line manager of employee relations for a large General Electric plant. She has been a consultant in marketing management development at GE and is currently vice president of services. She spends most of her time lecturing and supervising training courses, both inside and outside, of GE. All her working life has been with GE and her books are a distillation of a great deal of research and testing by GE in the areas covered by the book titles. Her books are not theory alone—they are theory which has been tested and which works.

Management Tasks, Responsibilities, Practices
Peter F. Drucker, Harper & Row, 1973.

Drucker has written many books. One of their great values is that they contain many of the ideas which Drucker developed as a result of his extensive consulting for top-flight companies, so that many of the thoughts and principles he writes about have been successfully applied.

McKinsey Foundation Lecture Series
Sponsored by GSB of Columbia University.

This series consists of lectures given by presidents and chief executive officers. One such is, "New Frontiers" by R. J. Cordiner, which describes GE's pioneering decentralization principles. Other authors include Blough, Greenewalt, Houser, Watson, and Kappel.

The American Challenge
  J. J. Servan Schreiber, Avon Books, 1969.
  A former best-seller in Europe and the United States by a prominent French journalist and politician. Interesting and valuable because it shows us as others see us.

The Lengthening Shadow: The Life of T. J. Watson
  T. and M. Belden, Little Brown & Company, 1962.
  This book is valuable to those who want a completely accurate story of IBM and T. J. Watson. The Beldens were commissioned by IBM to write the book and so all the facts are facts, at least as IBM sees them. It is a story of one of America's very greatest enterprises.

A final word on knowledge

The development of knowledge is aided greatly by an inquiring mind—the kind of attitude John Gardner speaks of in his book, *Self-Renewal.* For example, managers must not become smug or complacent, even if their company is in the industry leadership spot. IBM employees have this characteristic—none of them seem to believe that because they are first, they will always be first, and they work as hard as though they were trying to catch a front runner. This same inquiring attitude can be carried over in a positive way by asking, "What is my competitor doing better than I am? Is it product, delivery, service, price, or features?" It is too common to look for defects in competitors' offerings, rather than the good things they do. The former develops what may be a false sense of security; the latter encourages improvement.

One manager in a large company used to tell his home plant employees who traveled that they should always try to find an extra half day on the trip and use it to go through a company plant or a vendor's plant in the vicinity. He also asked for a very short report. He soon noticed that the reports usually pointed out all the things the other plant was doing in poorer fashion than their own plant. The manager then changed the required report to include only those things which the visited plant was doing better than the visitor's plant. Immediately the attitude of the traveling people changed—they now had to look for and find good ideas, and everybody benefited.

The scarcest element in almost any business enterprise is an adequate number of good-to-superior workers and managers who are motivated to do 5 percent better than average—and who do, in fact, year after year produce superior results. The absence of enough such people is the biggest challenge many managers face, namely: Can I construct a winning team out of average mortals? My answer is yes you can if you'll practice—with real enthusiasm—the seven managing principles in this book. This book is loaded with ideas and techniques to help you do so.

You as a boss, a leader, need to understand your people—have clear ideas as to what your mission is and to work cooperatively with your people. This requires that you be a good communicator. Communications—well handled—are a two-way street. You inform, explain, request, require, and you name it, *but* you also listen, understand and whenever possible act in ways that demonstrate your understanding and your desire to help your people realize their goals and ambitions.

Paul M. Hammaker

Good communications are indeed most important, but there must be substance to what is being communicated—strategy, objectives, standards of performance, time requirements—so that the listener is motivated to those things necessary for the company's well-being. Otherwise, communications are merely management by exhortation.

Louis T. Rader

5

Managing principle number three: Convey to your people what is wanted and then learn and consider what they think and want

If you are people sensitive (see Chapter 3) and if you have a good knowledge of your business, your industry, and the external environment (see Chapter 4), you possess two of the essentials for managing successfully. But they are not enough! A young manager needs also to be a good communicator. The ability to communicate is a managerial necessity. Managers achieve results by leading, directing, guiding, and inspiring others. The people reporting to the manager, whatever his level in the managerial ranks, do the work. They make the sales or the sail boats. They produce the reports or develop the new products. These—the producers—are not individual entrepreneurs doing as they see fit. They are part of an organization working within objectives, plans, budgets, and assigned responsibilities. These things are spelled out in the big picture, and broken down into specifics—tasks are assigned, progress monitored, and results recorded and evaluated. All of these things call for verbal and written communication.

Good managers are good communicators. Poor managers are most often poor communicators.

What does that really mean? It means that what is so lightly called communication is really the life line of management—the means by which resources are mobilized to achieve results. These resources may be thought of as existing in three major categories:

1. All the assets represented by invested money, land, plant and equipment, inventories, and receivables. These even in the automated factory are useless without people.

2. The products or services which the organization owns and offers. These include the products in development and production, the patents and copyrights. These are developed and put into production by people but do not constitute a business without the people to produce them and carry them to market.

3. The people who man the organization in every category from maintenance worker to president. They are really the significant resource when properly motivated and managed. Without them, all the investment in plant, equipment, and product is not worth much. With the same facilities the people decide whether the company will be a leader or a follower; whether it will be successful or go broke. A lot of lip service is given to this principle but a great number of managers do not seem to understand the absolute dependence there is on people performance. Most budgets which are made up, or cost-benefit analyses developed, have in their conclusions an assumption of major magnitude—that is, that there are people who will carry out the planned work. Experienced managers know that people can make any poor system work if they want to make it work, and make a good system fail if they want to make it fail. It's a demonstration of the old adage that you can lead a horse to water but you can't make him drink. You can employ people, but it takes communication and motivation to make them work productively for you.

Communication via job descriptions

The work people are to do is always discussed with them orally and sometimes followed up by a written job description. At the lowest hierarchical level, that of direct labor, the work can be completely specified and the workers can receive training to teach them the skills required. At higher levels, particularly if no physical work is involved, it is more difficult to specify the work to be done. In particular it is hard to specify interrelationships that may exist with other groups. Despite the greatest care and effort which may be exercised in trying to describe all the duties and relationships, the written approach is often most inadequate because it is both impossible and impractical to define every possible variation of work which may occur. Accordingly, an overall communication system is required which will give the employee enough information and motivation to enable him, and to stimulate him, to use his best judgment and energy to do what is good for the company, even though that has never been explicitly told to him.

The question being discussed here, then, is, "What are the fundamentals involved in getting people in the organization to do the job in the best interests of the company?" The answer is communication but there are several facets to this answer. A current popular phase is MIS or "management information system," which usually means utilizing computers and data processing to reduce all data required to run a business into a logical system to be of use to all levels of management. Although not graced with an equivalent phase like MCS, "management communication system," the communication system involved in running a business is very involved and extensive and important. It includes all modes of transmitting information, oral and written, manual or automatic, scheduled for immediate or later transmittal. The data may be for information only or contain rules, procedures, and orders for running the business. Some of these forms are:

Management communication system (MCS)

External

1. Official annual reports prepared for stockholders and special reports such as the 10K for the SEC.
2. In-house newspaper or magazine for all employees, usually carrying information judged to be of interest to the readers.
3. Press releases to local and national newspapers, radio, and TV aimed at the general public.
4. Advertising and sales promotion literature, or radio and TV programs aimed at possible customers.

Internal

5. Regular (weekly, monthly) operating results sent to a special mailing list.
6. Standard operating procedure in all functions.
7. Company policies, usually a static document to help guide managers.
8. Personnel job descriptions, evaluation reports for managers.
9. Boss talks to all employees or to groups.
10. Meetings of all kinds (staff, committees, operating groups, sales meeting for employees, sales meetings for customers).
11. In-house educational and training courses.
12. The boss walking through the shop or store or office.
13. Telephone, letters, telegraph between individuals or between groups.

Queries about MCS. The questions which a young manager should address himself to in the communication systems are: Is there such a thing as too much communication? Who is responsible for communicating and to whom? When should it be oral and when written? Is there any relationship between the communication system and morale or motivation?

MCS and employee attitude. There are many instances where employees gripe about their management and their company. Will a good communication system cure this unrest, criticism, bad attitude? The answer is no unless the information supplied is believed by the recipients. Do they believe what they hear? Only if they are quite sure or have reason to believe that the management and his employee relations people are quite honest and are giving all the relevant facts. If the people do not believe, for whatever reason, the communication is useless or even worse.

Can there be too much? Absolutely. Employees can get suspicious if they are flooded with a great deal of information. They begin to think that management is setting them up for something. Too much also often develops into paralyzing red tape.

What information should be transmitted? There is not a simple answer to this and yet it is a very important consideration. Should all employees be told if a company is losing money, and how much? If the answer is yes, then should they also be told if it is making good money? Should they be told of major complaints, liability suits, defective products as well as awards won, patents gained, market share gained? These questions should be thought through and resolved before an in-house publication is started or press releases are put out bragging about good corporate citizenship. There are, however, some simple ground rules:

1. The employee should be told by his supervisor anything about his company or his job which may give him cause for concern. He should not read in the local paper or from the union that some of his co-workers are to be laid off for lack of work before he has been told about it by his own management, or that the company is thinking of moving out of town, or of adding an addition, or that an employee was badly injured.

2. There must be a direct and continuous approach for combating rumors. They cannot be allowed to spread unchecked.

3. Employee attitudes should be monitored regularly to learn of their concerns and to discover weaknesses in the communication system.

MCS and meetings. In this century and particularly in the last 50 years, meetings have become an integral part of the managerial process. They are designed to accomplish a variety of purposes, some of which are information, problem exploration, decision making, morale building, planning, and budgeting.

Meetings can be valuable if certain rules are followed, or a great waste of time and money if improperly used. Our experience says that only 20 percent of all meetings we have ever attended were run efficiently, and many should not have been called at all. Some involve a very deliberate attempt by an inept (but politically inclined) person to transfer his responsibility to someone else or to a committee.

At the same time, they can be an important mechanism whereby young professionals get visibility, particularly with those in other functions or departments. Meetings can introduce the young trainee or young new manager to different problems of tremendous interest and value in the company and its environment. They can give him an opportunity for creative contribution to new or old problems, an opportunity to show his knowledge of the company, a chance to meet employees of equal or higher status from other functions.

Some rules for meetings

1. At the beginning of the meeting someone should ask, "What is the purpose of this meeting?" if the chairman does not indeed state the purpose. This is advisable because the call for the meeting is often received by phone or letter, but all the reasons are not explicitly stated or the time elapsed between call and meeting may considerably change the data or decisions required.

2. Generally, a supervisor and anyone reporting to him should not attend the same meeting unless it is known that both will be needed to make a necessary decision. If the meeting is primarily for communication, only one man is needed to carry the information.

3. Agreement should be rapidly reached on how elaborate the minutes should be. This can be done by chairman's decision. Usually a statement of one page or less of decisions arrived at is sufficient.

4. The old Army advice of "never volunteer" is the opposite of what makes sense for a young manager. Meetings form excellent sources for special assignments, usually of short duration and usually giving him contact with other functions.

5. If a meeting is for communications, the subordinates should help make up the agenda.

6. Should an invitee ever refuse to go to a meeting? Yes he should, particularly if it involves out-of-town travel and he is not certain there will be a net gain from it. It never hurts to ask his immediate supervisor for advice if there is any question about a meeting's value. This seems never to occur to some young men who, without thinking, attend everything they are invited to.

7. How often should meetings be held? When used as a mechanism for running a business, most general managers and functional managers hold meetings on regularly-set days once a week. There is great merit in a rigid schedule, even though some meetings may be very short.

ITT management meeting

Geneen of ITT has been both praised and lambasted in the press for his management techniques. One of them is the management meeting. A 90-foot long table is surrounded by some 80 high level executives every month in a management meeting. This is one of the most publicized mechanisms used by Geneen of ITT as the major method of control and communication. The average length of time of the top executive away from his office is probably two days. The preparation time for the questions and answers is at least the same. The meeting itself often lasts two days. Is it worth it? Every month?

And what does Geneen get? He gets:

Direct answers from his major executives to direct questions, no staff is in between. The executive either knows the answer to questions on sales, net, inventory turnover, future prospects, or if he doesn't, both Geneen and all his peers know that he doesn't.

Every executive gets some idea each month of progress and problems in each of the other divisions.

Cooperation—to help each other or contribute ideas to solutions of problems—is made easy or at least possible.

Interactions before and after the main meeting allow participants to resolve problems or raise issues between any two or more components.

Everyone gets the word as to what company policy is in any area. There is little ambiguity as to what the working rules are. They hear what are the main problems facing any division or the company and what the possible solutions might be.

Summary

Most managers are at least average in their ability to communicate. One reason for this is that poor communicators are rarely hired or promoted into the managerial ranks. To test the importance of this attribute we asked over 500 quite successful middle managers to appraise their own ability in this field. They all felt they were superior communicators and on the average believed that one third of their pay could be attributed to this capability.

Managers can improve their communicating skills—both oral and written—if they merely realize those skills' importance and decide to improve. Many graduate schools of business have mandatory courses to make certain their graduates meet certain qualifications in oral and written communications.

Effective communications cannot exist if there is not complete integrity in the system. People are not stupid. The old saying is so true, "What you do speaks so loudly I cannot hear what you are saying." The Latins compressed it into the simple *"Facta non verba"*—"Deeds not words"—but in today's world both are needed. Good deeds and good words are a difficult combination to beat.

The ability of young managers to deal effectively with people is an almost absolute requisite for success in virtually every business. Effective dealings revolve around the example set by the young manager, his understanding of his people via listening with care to their communications to him and his ideas, objectives, plans, messages. Almost every manager is in the communications business, just as surely as are newspapers, magazines, and TV. Usually the manager's task requires greater objectivity, greater accuracy, greater integrity than that evidenced by many reporters, editors, and commentators.

Those who think and dream and hope and those who have fine character and personalities *but* don't make it happen can rarely, if ever, be successful managers. The single most important thing against which managers are measured is—Did they make it happen? Stated differently, did they meet the goal? Pertinent to this is the query, did they make or follow the plan which was the basis for believing the goal could be met?

We surely need in our society thinkers and dreamers and citizens of fine character. When they have managerial responsibility and achieve or exceed the business goal set—when they make it happen—they are excellent managers. Such managers are in short supply, and therein lies the great opportunity for young managers with the will and wit to develop themselves to become super-good managers.

Paul M. Hammaker

There is a perfectly legitimate functional area called business planning. I would never entrust this responsibility to plan for the future to a person who had not already demonstrated he could run a business today. Planning, either short- or long-range, done by people who do not know clearly the constraints on the business, is merely an escape from reality.

Louis T. Rader

6

Managing principle number four: Plan what is to be done and make it happen

All managers young or old must do some planning. They may do so consciously or unconsciously, formally or informally, and either on a day-to-day basis or for a longer time span. One important determinant of the degree of success a manager achieves is the relative soundness of his planning; another is how well his plans are implemented. A good plan plus good implementation equals good performance. The effectiveness of the sum total of the plans and their implementation by all managers represents the effectiveness of the business.

Almost everyone agrees—in principle, at least—that a plan is a necessary road map for a business to specify the actions necessary to take the organization from where it is to a desired destination. Two of the major considerations are the environment and the time factor.

If the environment in which an organization operated were static, there would be little need for plans, but the modern world is anything but static and products are continually threatened by new developments. The buggy-whip manufacturer is usually held up as the classic case to demonstrate change and the sometimes fatal result of failing to adjust to change. There are scores of other examples, many of which the reader could cite.

In addition to factors such as innovations, competitors' actions, social forces, changing consumer preferences, money supply, government regulations, and others which are usually referred to as environmental, another major consideration is that of time. It takes a lot of time to get things done. To put a new product into production may take from six months to five years, depending on the amount of development required and the market testing done. Not only does development take time, but so does the planning and building of new facilities, the hiring and training of workers, the establishment of sales outlets.

Managers are paid in part to "know the future." To do an acceptable job for their business, then, they must know a great deal about the factors affecting their business and the capabilities of their company, which includes their people and financial resources, to plan for the future.

Good planning involves a great deal of analysis—of the total environment, of a component's strengths and weaknesses, of alternative steps that could be followed. But the first major point we wish to make is that planning is not an objective in itself. It is merely a means to an end. It is for that reason we include in the title of this chapter, "make it happen." Too many young professional managers, especially MBAs, tend to miss this distinction. They may be excellent at "planning" a job, but they do not feel that it is any measure of their competence whether or not the plans are executed. They continue to study and re-plan, and are not really concerned with the execution of the plan. They often give the kind of answer which infuriates a result-oriented top manager: "I did my job, I gave him the plan. It's no fault of mine that he didn't carry it out, but if you wish, I'll make another plan." This, because planning often rests on detailed analyses, gives rise to what has been called "paralysis by analysis." This means that too many people in the organization have confused analysis and resulting plans with results. Laudable as is the IBM admonition "THINK" is, it has given rise to another slogan which points out the necessity for not taking the IBM slogan too literally as being a complete answer. The authors believe in managing and planning a time comes when it is advisable to "Stop Thinking and Do Something."

Along with analysis go assumptions. What are the assumptions about future new product introduction, competitors' actions, pricing, consumer behavior and all matters where some type of conclusion or expectation undergirds a plan?

One of the most rigorous engineering courses in industry trains its men on the basis of writing a problem statement first, which is as complete as can be developed, and then outlining all the assumptions which are made in order to obtain an analytical solution. This approach forces the student to realize that there are assumptions inherent in every equation he writes, and so he realizes that answers obtained—even if a computer is used—may be correct only if the assumptions are good. Another way of saying this is that the biggest mistakes are made when the assumptions are no good. This is a good procedure to follow in making out a one-year budget, or five-year plan. Assumptions such as the current recession (or boom) will end in one year, or the economy will continue to grow at 3 percent or 8 percent a year, or there will be no new laws enacted to upset import opportunities, and so forth, make one aware of the fantastic number of variables which can affect a business—political and social, as well as economic.

All levels of management, whether explicitly stated or not, have planning as a part of their job requirement. Some management experts believe that at the general manager level on a decentralized operation, about 50 percent of the manager's time should be devoted to planning. Above that level (i.e., at the group or company level), an even higher percentage of time is demanded for this function. Similarly, at levels below the general manager, less time as a percentage is allocated to planning, but it is still an appreciable amount. It is an observation of the authors that if the GM spends 50 percent of his time planning, then the managers reporting to him should devote about 30 percent of their's to it, the next level around 20 percent, and the next 10 percent. This is a very rough rule of thumb, but it says that if planning is that important for the success of the general manager (which means for the business), then it is also quite important for the levels which report to him. The percentages given above for planning time allocation are approximately the same as the ratio of salaries paid those levels in many companies; that is, a functional manager will have a base pay about 60 percent that of his bosses' and the level reporting to him a salary equal to 60 percent to 65 percent of his.

Staff versus line

Unfortunately, many managers relegate planning to the back burner because they are so concerned with the day-to-day running of the business they do not believe planning is that important. Fire fighting takes all their time and to them planning is something to be done with the left hand while the right hand is fully occupied. Over short periods of time there is little harm done by this; however, if extended over a long period, the business will suffer because trends will not be identified soon enough and appropriate action not initiated in time. If the business suffers, it must reflect on the manager no matter how unusual the incidents which impact the business. In retrospect, many of the unusual factors cast a shadow before them and were discernible in advance had the manager looked, talked, discussed, thought, and conjectured.

Another approach to planning is to have it done in a staff environment. Unfortunately too many young managers feel this is a desirable job too soon in their careers. Good planning above all else can utilize experience, and that's the one thing a bright young manager does not have. We believe he should work in at least two functional areas before he opts for planning. Staff planning has several inherent liabilities. One is that staff must depend on line people for a great deal of information and line people often—if not usually—view planners with suspicion unless they happen to be personal friends. The implementation of the planning then depends on a usually tortuous route through the manager-planning who, supported by the boss, more or less consistently works with the line people to persuade them to buy the plan. Since planning is erroneously deemed to be an exciting, free-wheeling job without many constraints, it is too often true that salesmen or engineers who find quotas or other measurements too onerous get into planning. For these, planning is an escape from reality. We believe no one should be allowed to be in a staff planning position who does not have a proven record of success behind him.

Objectives

Companies are supposed to have objectives. We believe they really exist in a fully meaningful way only if they are in writing. If they are not, then only a few at the higher levels know what they are. Planning at the higher levels is directed toward the realization of those objectives and certainly it is easier for all in the organization when these are clear-cut and well known to all planners and doers.

There are some who believe that the whole philosophy of management is dependent on written objectives at every level and for every executive person whose performance should be measured. This is known as management by objectives (MBO). We have no quarrel with the concept except that we think too much is claimed for it. There are also many actions which are favorable to a company's well-being which cannot be spelled out in advance in the form of an objective. Well-motivated employees deal conscientiously with such matters—though they are not formal objectives. When too much emphasis is on MBO new problems may be neglected.

At every level below the top there should be functional plans which support the master plan of the business. The master plan has both a short-range part known as the annual budget and a long-range part which often goes out three to five years. The various functions or components of an organization should have their own plans which mesh with and support the organization plan, in both short- and long-range. There should, then, be an engineering plan, a manufacturing plan, a marketing plan, a finance plan, and an employee and public relations plan. They should include as appropriate such things as innovations, market share improvement, product features, productivity, and personnel training as well as the usual budgetary data. In fact the plans should include as a minimum all the key result areas outlined in the measurement Chapter 7.

Plan? Yes! Then make it happen

1. The good IBM "THINK" slogan has precipitated a counter: "Stop Thinking and Do Something."

2. The adage, "If it's worth doing, it's worth doing well," should be replaced by, "If it's worth doing, *do it!*"

3. In this day of advanced education and a constant harping on more and more education, many people have gotten in a mode which can be called "paralysis by analysis." They analyze and quit—or make a plan and don't put it into effect.

4. Two professions—medical and military—must make decisions as to what to do very rapidly—they can't wait for more data, or go to study a book, but have to decide what to do and do it. As a result they often develop remarkable intuitive decision-making processes.

5. There are only a few crucial business decisions made in a senior manager's life. However, in lower management levels less important but still significant decisions are needed and made frequently. Some need to be made at once, but many permit from several days to several months for investigation, analysis, and conclusions.

Most successful corporations have a good record of making sound, critical decisions—though they may be few in number. Sears is an interesting example, and its decisions of a basic nature are unusually well documented. Over a span of 40 years, a limited number of crucial decisions explain in part how Sears became the world's greatest merchandising institution. The 10 critical decisions were:

a. In mid-twenties decided to add retail stores.

b. The decision to centralize merchandising in Chicago and to control store operations from territorial (regional) headquarters.

c. The decision to control the cost and quality of merchandise by having it made to Sears specifications. Buy on "known cost" basis.

d. The sweeping decision after World War II to expand aggressively.

e. The decision in the mid-50s to expand sales of soft goods and become full line department stores.

f. The more recent decision to play up style and fashion along with economy.

g. The decision to set up a service organization, despite its low or zero profitability, to support the sales of durable goods.

h. The decision to diversify into insurance.

i. The decision to invest in supplier corporations.

j. Finally, a decision to invest heavily in superior personnel.

Large-scale training program.

Generous profit-sharing plan. (Sears employee profit-sharing fund owns about 26 percent of Sears common stock.)

Result: Sears has superior management.[1]

Not all of these decisions were sharply defined as of a given moment. Some took years of evolution. Some flowed naturally out of others. Sears' success is rooted in people and organization. The basic idea of the present organization—centralized merchandising and decentralized administration of stores—was outlined on paper in 1929, *almost 20 years before it was fully adopted.* It was originally proposed by Sears committee on organization, tried briefly, and abandoned during the 30s due to:

Difficulty in finding able territorial administrators.
Friction between central merchants in Chicago and territorial administrators.
General Wood feared the growth of territorial bureaucracies.
Depression cut sales—expense considerations led to disbanding territories.

Then, Sears tried one central merchandising office and hundreds of stores reporting to the president, but this was no solution to the problem. The next step following this was the development of big-city groupings. Following this, the West Coast was set up as a territory in 1940, responsible for both store and catalog operation. After World War II, four more similar territories were set up so that there are now five territories—each run by a vice president.

6. There are some who believe American colleges are

---

[1] Based on information in the May 1964 issue of *Fortune Magazine;* © 1964 Time Inc.

developing the cult of the nonleader–people who feel that it is more important and valuable to criticize others who try to do something rather than to try to do it themselves. Most of our big city newspapers fall in this class. Brilliant writers, incisive critics who can find fault with anything–even the kind of carriage a Pope might ride in—and yet who will not venture into the arena of public service themselves. The small town newspapers are usually the opposite. They identify with the local civic and charitable and religious leaders and help to make good things happen.

7. In business, although planning is necessary and important, unless one is in the planning-consulting business or a service business, the item which is sold by manufacturers and retailers is not a plan but a physical product. And that product has to be produced at competitive costs, with competitive features and acceptable quality offered at a price that causes the purchaser to want it more than the money it costs.

8. Manufacturing industries have a small infinity of problems which occur as a product goes into manufacturing. Having a patent and a set of engineering drawings may mean very little to success. Someone with judgment and determination has to carry the manufacturing procedures through to completion, much as a machete-wielder cuts his way through a jungle. Someone has to want to make it happen and these someones are usually aggressive manufacturing men. All they have to be convinced of is that the product can be built and will work.

Sometimes the suspicion exists that engineers deem themselves a success when the product is theoretically manufacturable but practically impossible to build.

9. In the same way that it is said a fool can ask more questions in a minute than a wise man can answer in a month, so in the business world of either services or manufacturing goods there are so many possible deterrents to performance that many just give up or take it easy and blame the weather, government, competitors, environment, fellow workers or whatever, as an excuse for nonperformance.

10. All of the plans in the world are merely interesting collections of words and ideas and are nothing more than mental exercise *until* and *unless* they are put into effect. A manager's job includes planning and making it happen.

11. After a plan—thought to be good and well-implemented—fails, is that the end of the ball game? It shouldn't be. Why did the plan fail?

A manager at the Summer Six Week Executive Program given by the Darden Graduate Business School said:

This may be more of a technical process or methodology than "management technique," but I have found that a rather searching "post mortem" of all the elements involved (and by those involved in its generation) of a failed project is beneficial to our group. A failed project in my business is generally a dry hole or an unsuccessful workover of an oil or gas well. In the case of a dry hole, the gut reaction is often to forget it as soon as possible and get on with the next test or development well. A good "wring out" of all the elements (subsurface geology, geophysics, etc.) insures that we learn more from this venture than the fact that it was dry. These are not blame-fixing sessions, but are sincere efforts to *help avoid* making the same error or errors again. Involvement in conception and birth (or death of the well if dry) by staff *and* management is necessary and mutually beneficial.

What about new young managers and planning?

The first question is: Does your boss expect you to plan? If so, what are you to plan? Many young managers plan such things as the clerical reduction permitted by a new systems installation, the number of salespeople needed for a coming sale of mens' shirts, the scheduling of receipts for a rather even work flow, a plan for reducing the average age of accounts receivables, the development of economic order quantities, a way of informing production workers of each day's output, and the cumulative month-to-date production compared with the plan.

If you are to plan and you know what to plan, you have some choices.

If your predecessor had a method, do you want to follow it permanently? If not, where and how can you search for other ways of doing it? Or, how can you gather data, assess the variables, and create a new better method?

If your job does not call for planning, is that all there is to it? Should you delve into your total responsibility and see if unpredicted and costly happenings occur. If they do, why? The probable reason is no one foresaw a difficulty, it was expected all would go smoothly. Or even worse, there may exist the belief that some things are sure to go wrong, regardless of what anyone does or can do.

Many a young manager has enhanced his opportunities by finding different, new, better ways to do a job. If you think of such an improvement and want to put it into effect, you frequently will go through the following steps:

1. State what has been the method.
2. Though it has merit, these specific weaknesses have developed.
3. A way to overcome the major and/or most costly weaknesses.
4. What to do, how to do it, when to do it, who will do it, its cost, who it will affect, how? Are all the elements to consider and deal with *in* your plan for improvement?
5. Present the plan persuasively (with no criticism of the past) as an opportunity for the company to benefit. If you can do so comfortably, you may add that it should add to the department's and your boss's reputation. In addition, if it is sincere and you can do so gracefully, you may wish to add that your interest in the success of the department and/or company is what stimulated you into thinking about this and then working out a plan.
6. Have your boss explain the plan with your assistance to all who will be affected, or get his permission for you to handle it and do a combination—he to cover the plan with certain people, and you to cover the plan with others.
7. Work out with your boss's help, if needed, when the plan is to go into effect and who is responsible for each part.
8. Work out a reporting system so that progress or failure can be measured on the key elements of the plan on a regular basis.
9. Evaluate results. Be guided by what they tell you, particularly where further thinking, planning work needs to be done.

In all planning, it is desirable to learn:

1. What happened last week, last month, or last year.
2. If for the planning period everything is not sure to be unchanged, what might change?
3. Now that you have the variables, do you want to change anything under your control? If so, what, why, when?

4. If you don't want to change any variables, which ones will change, or do you think might change? A wage increase going into effect next month, for instance, is usually known and should be factored into your plans.

In the Coca Cola bottling business, the price of syrup is set by quarters by the parent company. In a time of fluctuating sugar prices the manager, young or old, who is planning costs should make his best estimate of future quarter prices (probably the next four). He should state what assumptions led him to his conclusion. This enables his boss to feed in his ideas, which may be of great value to the young manager. In any event, if his boss accepts the young manager's conclusions, at least they're regarded as reasonable.

Advice from the authors

Don't get mousetrapped into a budget that is just based on rough forecasted numbers, whether yours, your boss's, or his boss's.

Do understand the variables in your operation. Do a skillful estimating job of the effect, favorable and unfavorable, on the factors beyond your control. Believe that enough of the significant factors are under your control so you know you can manage these variables. (If you can't manage many significant factors, wherein are you a manager?)

Your plans for doing certain things better should be given an appropriate plus figure, whether you are dealing with costs, discounts, margins, sales in dollars or sales in product units, such as cases of Coca Cola.

Then, considering the factors that will likely go against you—plus the favorable factors you intend to create—you are ready to put down numbers reflecting your planning that can and should become the budget you want to go on the line for and say you will accomplish. You need then to follow through.

Make it happen

Following are observations from ten practical, operating managers dealing with management by objectives, goals, improvement programs, and planning:

On management by objectives (one manager's ideas). Management by objectives (MBO) has proven to be a successful technique for achieving results, while giving a manager an opportunity to exercise his abilities freely. A manager frequently measures success only in terms of salary and advancement. Once he has reached the level of his capabilities in an organization and has progressed to top salary scales, how can he succeed further? MBO gives him the ability to measure his success in meeting his own goals, as negotiated with his boss. The individual also writes his own appraisal relative to his objectives. It therefore gives each manager the opportunity to succeed (or fail) in doing what he sets out to do. Used properly, it can motivate individuals who otherwise could "die in place."

On management by objectives (a second manager's ideas). The past several years now our company has been using the technique of management by objectives; however, this primarily concerned corporate and departmental objectives. Rarely were the first-line supervisors (noncontract) aware of these objectives, even though they made contributions in their efforts.

This year in our department, middle and first-line supervisors were made fully aware of department objectives and additionally were requested to submit individual objectives for themselves. These were to be objectives that could be measured.

The submission of these individual objectives proved to be an enlightenment for the department management as it gave them a feel for the concern of this particular group and additionally it exposed areas of improvement that will contribute to the well-being of the company.

On management by objectives (a third manager's ideas). The establishment of goals for each individual in the marketing services department has been most successful. All employees, *including stenos,* are requested to formulate 5-10 specific goals for accomplishment during the year. I review and agree to the employee's written goals and these become a basis for evaluation of the employee's performance during and at the end of the year. This process has the following advantages:

1. The employee determines the goal, so no problems are

encountered with unreasonable goals (some are more difficult than I would assign).

2. The employee strives to make the goal.
3. The written goal gives me an insight as to how the employee sees his job in regard to priorities, etc.
4. The goals provide a system for accountability.

On goals (a fourth manager's ideas). We set goals or objectives for the department managers and keep them competing with each other on these goals. If they meet these goals or fail, this is discussed with them on quarterly reviews. We have found this has been very successful.

On profit improvement programs (a fifth manager's ideas). Our company has what I feel to be a very effective tool, used in both manufacturing and merchandising. We call it "Profit Improvement Program." Basically, it is a means of setting goals and plans for attaining goals, each year and revising each quarter.

Goals are set on each element of cost where supervisors, department heads, plant managers, and so forth, can affect change. Individuals set their own goals.

This program allows every level of management to participate in a very aggressive program of cost reduction. Too, each individual knows from weekly, quarterly, and annual reviews exactly the personal performance. We have found that our management people really see this as a cost "road map" to their job.

The dollar accomplishments have been very rewarding and contribute heavily to company profits.

On operations improvement programs (a sixth manager's ideas). One management technique that has been very effective for me has been an operations improvement program (OIP) that has been primarily directed at all levels of supervision within our operating plants. This program is based on the question of how can an operation be improved in respect to efficiency, cost, quality, flow, employee relations or comfort, and so forth.

Each level of supervision is thoroughly briefed on how this program is administered by the plant manager. The plant manager is directly involved in this program from its beginning and thus sets the tone for all management personnel. Goals are

established within each department by the concerned departmental manager within his department where he feels improvement can be made. When he identifies these areas, priorities are
set and a feasibility study is made by the supervisor, the department head, and the OIP coordinator, who is usually the industrial engineer at the plant level. When completed, the study is
reviewed by the plant superintendent and the plant manager and
implementation is begun if the suggestion proves feasible. If the
suggestion does not meet the feasibility criteria, it is thoroughly
explained to the supervisor who suggested it in order that he
understand why it will not be followed up. I might add that
very few of the suggestions prove to be unacceptable. If the
suggestion is implemented, the results involved are made a
permanent part of this supervisor's file and consequently taken
into consideration on his performance review (which, by the
way, he is aware of).

This approach, while not unique, seems to add new life to the
supervisor's approach to management of his department. This
approach has proven to be very effective at the plant level and
should apply to any level within a corporation.

*On improvements and accomplishments (a seventh manager's
ideas).* I require plant managers and department managers to set
goals of savings and improvements they will make during the
year through innovation, improved process changes, and so forth.
We then measure results monthly. Competition between the men
is encouraged and has resulted in significant savings.

I require staff heads to give me written reports on Monday
morning of what they and their associates accomplished the
previous week. This improved staff efficiency and helped organize and conclude work that had a tendency to be drawn out.

I occasionally jot down what I did for a day. I usually realize
that my time is not being spent doing what I should be doing.

I make it a point to compliment each person who reports to
me once a week on a genuine good accomplishment. The compliment must be a real and sincere one to be effective.

On planning (an eighth manager's ideas). A management
technique which I feel is very effective is one which is practiced
by my boss. I think many managers and supervisors in my
company give a good deal of lip service to planning, setting goals

and objectives, reviewing progress and deficiencies, and so forth, but fewer practice it in an effective way. There are forms which employers and supervisors are supposed to complete in this regard. We do not use the form in my department. We are asked simply to outline in memo form—from us to the boss—what we expect to accomplish during the year. Each quarter the boss reviews with us, individually, this plan and our progress, not only from the standpoint of the plan, but how we are progressing in general. I always know exactly where I stand.

Coupled with this is an atmosphere, generated by the boss, of really feeling a responsibility and accountability for what I am doing. On the other hand, the atmosphere is one in which I feel that making a mistake is not going to be the end of the world, and most times it turns out to be a real, positive learning experience because of the very positive way it is handled by the boss.

On planning (a ninth manager's ideas). The one major problem that bothered me the most was the lack of a truly coordinated budget and plan. After three years of trying to get our department to do one, I sat back and tried to figure out why I wasn't getting anywhere. It then struck me that my vice president probably wanted one but he, too, did not know how to really go about getting one. I therefore got my group together and drew up a formal method for setting up a plan and budget from the plan and finally how to control both of them. I then proceeded to feed this information to my boss on a piecemeal basis so that he could think it over in his own mind and not be confounded with a new idea without knowing any details. I also had two others of my group talk to him to discuss it and showed him how I had done mine for the next two years and suggested that he might wish to use this as a basis for planning his own goals. The end result was that the entire department must now prepare a formal plan and tie it to the budget. The lesson I learned was that he was waiting for someone to come forward with the whole idea laid out for him so he could evaluate it and not have one prepared by him that might not be accepted by the people below him.

On joint planning (a tenth manager's ideas). A management technique that I have seen successfully employed is departmental "joint planning sessions."

Yearly, during the fall, preliminary plans are submitted by department for manpower/budgeting during the following year. In December the allocations are made by department and by January the actual budget and plans must be in place.

Several departments recently have utilized group planning sessions by all department management. All go away from the office and over several days discuss fully all aspects and alternatives and must arrive at decisions that are fully acceptable to the group.

The result is a comprehensive, prioritized, cohesive departmental plan based on the interaction and interrelationships established by discussion and contention. The preliminary plan is submitted. Upon allocation a review meeting is conducted to review the plan and finalize necessary changes to the "team game plan."

The cooperatively, mutually established goals and programs have complete understanding of mission and responsibilities built in to them and receive good support from those who developed them.

The measuring of results against a plan or goal can be a positive motivating force. People do best those things they are measured on. Lack of measurement, or the sloppy use of data, reports, results designed to show success or failure in achieving the goals set, deprive a manager and his people of a strong motivating element. This is especially true related to people who do not possess strong self-motivation.

Paul M. Hammaker

It's been said over and over again and it's always true—people do best in those areas where they are measured. And the measurement must be objective, preferably by a number. Engineers all over the world subscribe to Lord Kelvin's statement in 1883: "I often say that when you can measure what you are talking about, and express it in numbers, you know something about it; but when you cannot measure it, when you cannot express it in numbers, your knowledge is of a meagre and unsatisfactory kind. . . ."

Louis T. Rader

7

Managing principle number five: Measure results and control operations through a reporting system

All managers, young or old, are faced with the task of measuring what has happened related to what was planned—or if not planned, what was desired or hoped for. Another task facing them is to evaluate the effectiveness of those who were charged with making it happen—making the plan work. A third task, when results are not satisfactory, is to devise and put into effect a new plan or a better method or an improved procedure.

In the management of a business, the ideal control system used is one which develops goal congruence on the part of the employees and the company. That is, the control system attempts to motivate the employees to do what is best for achieving the company's goals. In this environment the measurement system must be an aid to decision making, not a substitute for it. Everyone recognizes the need for measurements in business, just as they know that a scoring system is essential for sports such as baseball, football, or tennis, and a mileage gauge is desirable for an automobile. In many companies, the most comprehensive and detailed document developed is the annual budget. This usually takes many, many hours to prepare and to get top management approval of it. It then becomes the benchmark against which everything is measured.

It is unfortunately true that a company can achieve a budget for several years in a row and still go bankrupt. There are other factors in a business which a purely "mercenary" approach like a budget will not define or control or identify. These are factors such as employee morale, product quality, adherence to relevant laws, new designs, good R&D—none of which appear directly as a number item in a budget, but which can affect the business significantly in the long run.

In 1952 General Electric established a measurements project to study and define those measurements required to enable it to properly measure performances especially in a decentralized organization. This work has been well recorded.[1] The project was divided into three major subareas:

1. Operational measurements of the results of a business—at that time called a "product department."
2. Functional measurements—for example, engineering, manufacturing, marketing, employee relations, legal.
3. Measurements of the work of managing, as such.

Under operational measurements, eight key result areas were identified, decided on, and became part of GE practice. They are:

1. Profitability.
2. Market position.
3. Productivity.
4. Product leadership.
5. Personnel development.
6. Employee attitudes.
7. Public responsibility.
8. Balance between short-range and long-range goals.

These were developed on the basis that continued failure in any one area would jeopardize the component's future, even though all the other key areas had good results.

The above has stood the test of the last 20 years and is a

---

[1] See R. J. Cordiner, *New Frontiers for Professional Managers* (McGraw-Hill Book Company, Inc., 1956), and R. N. Anthony, John Dearden, and R. F. Vancil, *Management Control Systems* (Richard D. Irwin, Inc., 1972), pp. 137-45.

good illustration of a major point—namely, that no one measurement can adequately portray the health or situation of a business. Within each of the above major categories there are many specific measurements called for.

The time interval varies considerably. For profitability and productivity, the usual interval is monthly for internal reporting, and quarterly for external or public reporting. All the others are usually calculated annually, since there are often many seasonal and cyclical factors which tend to make more frequent evaluations not too meaningful. At the manufacturing level some companies may measure output, shipments, and billings on a daily basis.

The measurements which historically have had maximum emphasis and exposure are those of profitability—these get high visibility in the business press and are well known indices. They include net profit after tax as a percentage of sales; net profit as a return on investment, inventory turnover, current ratio, cash flow, operating ratio, depreciation, interest, earnings per share, and price earnings ratio. Nearly all manufacturing and retail companies use these or very similar measurements.

Several points should be noted, however. Very few measurements have significance when standing alone. They must be compared to something to have value. That "something" is usually the budget, or the previous year's performance for the same time period, or the competition.

Profitability cannot usually be compared between different kinds of businesses. What is a good net profit ratio to sales for a chemical company would be meaningless if compared to the same ratio realized by a supermarket chain. The return on assets employed is perhaps the most applicable and most commonly used measurement.

In the functional areas, for example, manufacturing, the best comparison is against prior years, preferably going back at least five years. These historical data reflect accurately the unique conditions which affect an operation such as local taxes, local pay rates, transportation costs, and—unless there has been a major change in a variable such as product mix or plant capacity—reflect accurately the trend line of cost and productivity. Management must be concerned with trends as much as absolute measurements. If the trend is bad, trouble is foreseen, and vice versa.

Because standards are different for different kinds of business (e.g., manufacturing vs. banking vs. hospitals), it is necessary that the young manager learn as soon as possible what the most significant measurements are for his particular business. These are best learned by asking his supervisors what they believe are the most useful measurements, but not stopping there. It may be that published industry data show additional or different measurements, and it is well to know what these are, and to apply them to the business.

Because the environment within which a business operates is changing all the time, it is necessary to assess continually the major factors affecting a business and to look at the measurement system to see if it should be modified. For example, many years ago, carload freight-loadings was one very good index of industrial activity. As intercity truck traffic grew, however, the significance and importance of carloadings changed. Similarly, as housing starts are identified, the question has to be asked as to whether mobile homes are included or not, and whether other factors such as the building of apartments or condominiums has changed its validity as an economic index.

In much more major fashion, government activities such as OSHA, EEO, and the Pension Reform Act (ERISA) have introduced new restraints on business and it is most important that the business conform. When should their impact be reflected in the measurement system?

Ten years ago very few companies measured what percentage of their employees belonged to disadvantaged and minority groups. Today, in some businesses, particularly those seeking government contracts, this is of great significance.

Similarly, in manufacturing industries, the question of quality control has assumed greater importance because of consumerism, government reliability standards, and customer lawsuits. Accordingly, for internal control purposes, many companies now call for various operating quality costs in appraisal, prevention, internal and external failures which were unheard of 20 years ago.

In the early days of manufacturing, say about 1900, the average manufacturing company had about 80 percent of its total employment in people who were making and assembling the product. There were very few engineering, marketing, or finance people. Accordingly, the measurement system grew up around direct labor, and even though the direct labor content has dropped in many cases to 5 percent to 10 percent of the sales dollar, the same base is still being used. Even where direct labor is low, all manufacturing costs (including purchased material, parts, and services) amount to around 60 percent. Since more of the sales dollar is under the control of manufacturing, it is perhaps not out of line that most measurements are of that function. This is unfortunate in many respects, however, because both engineering and marketing significantly affect the profitability and growth of a business, but there are few if any measurements to show this impact and to help judge the function as being good or poor.

Both engineering and marketing involve a fair degree of creativity in the product planning and design phases as well as in marketing strategy. It is unfortunately true that it is hard to develop measurements of creativity other than intuitive or subjective ones. The problem is that if creativity is involved, no one knows whether the problem that was given a person, or a group of people, was indeed capable of solution, and so in many cases the measurement drops down to a best effort—of a reasonably bright person who works reasonably hard. The same state of affairs exists to some extent in marketing. It is easy to give a salesman a quota to get so much business at a certain price within an assigned area and within a certain time. If, however, the salesman is faced with a large number of intangibles and is also supposed to develop new customers, the true measurement of his performance may not be correctly judged merely by the attainment of his quota. This remains as a major challenge in the field of measurements.

Although not usually discussed as such, the measurement of people's performance can rarely be divorced from their component's performance. If the component does well, everybody looks good, as on a winning sport team. If the component does poorly, it is hard for the manager to look good. It is for this

reason that ambitious young men should weigh carefully the
risks involved in going into a very difficult business situation.
Sometimes they become heroes, but more often conditions
beyond their control can put a dent into their careers. For
unfortunately, higher-level management who have allowed a
situation to deteriorate until drastic action is necessary (such as
changing the management) rarely appreciate how bad a situation
may be and both how hard it is and how long it may be before
it can be turned around. Businesses, like flywheels, have a great
deal of momentum and cannot quickly be changed. A general
rule is that if it takes x years for a company to get sick, it will
take about the same number of years to make it well, despite
aggressive, new leadership.

Since measurements are usually against goals or budgets, it
should be pointed out that goals which are too high are self-
defeating because they appear impossible to the participant.
Even though many high-level managers feel that their people
always have an extra 20 percent of effort to give, they seem to
forget that this does not seem to be true again and again after
the extra effort has been obtained once. At the same time, goals
which are too low are counterproductive.

Unfortunately, some top management seems to believe that
the only way to control a business is to install more and more
measurements. This gives rise to what is known as red tape or
bureaucratic strangulation. The government is perhaps the best
example of this.

It is in this area that young and alert managers can make a
contribution to their company and to themselves. Instead of
accepting blindly all requests for measurements, old and new,
they can do some analysis and make suggestions upward which
could have the effect of cutting out old, useless (or nonmeaning-
ful) measurements in favor of much more useful ones. To do
this, however, takes fundamental analysis and then salesmanship.

This problem has become very much more acute in recent
years because of the computer and automated data processing.
More and more information is being spewed out, much of it
useless. Very few managers have the guts to say so, and to clash
head-on with the data processing expert who says it doesn't cost
any more to get all this extra data. A very simple rule on

obtaining data is to establish how much time is spent on the average in appraising or utilizing it. If the latter is small the odds are great that the data should not have been collected.

Budgets

Budgets are probably the most common management tool. Many questions can be asked about the budget, what it means, and the importance management ascribes to it. The approach may be different in different companies, or even within different components of the same company. There are several different ways of looking at a budget. Some of these are:

1. The budget is an absolutely firm commitment to top management by the people who submit it. There is no excuse allowed for not adhering to it. Managers are expected to overcome unfavorable situations and to use ingenuity to achieve budgeted figures. The bigger the company, the more usual is this approach, and this is logical because in a big company, such as General Electric, there are many levels of budgets, all of which depend for results on those which feed them. For example, a division budget is made up of several department budgets; a group budget is made up of the sum of several divisions; the company budget which the chief executive officer submits to the board is made up of the sum of the groups. Under these conditions it is reasonable for top management to consider a budget as a very firm commitment.

2. Some companies look on the budget as a best effort commitment, and even allow the budget to be changed during the year. In this system if new factors develop which were unforeseen at budget-making time—such as foreign competition, inflation or recession—the manager can say, "I did my best, there were too many things over which I had no control," and these excuses are acceptable.

3. A third approach to a budget is to establish it with a 90 percent assurance of success at the time of making. This means that there is some stretch, but a reasonable chance of making it.

When it becomes evident that the original budget cannot be achieved, new figures can be submitted as estimates tied to certain dates. For example, the budget made out in December

for the following year, may call for earnings of $200,000. A
March estimate may specify $190,000, and a September estimate
$180,000. The final performance for the year may be $180,000,
which is considered 90 percent of budget, even though it makes
the September estimate. It is very dangerous to allow the March
or September estimates to be referred to as "new" budget
figures, or motivation ceases to make the original.

A budget which has no stretch or no growth is useless for a
good company and is not a motivating force. But a budget
which has too much stretch and appears unattainable is also
counter-motivating. The making of a good budget, then, is a
most important task. There must be some challenge in it to
motivate all participants and yet it cannot be impossible to
achieve.

A common technique is to specify all the major assumptions
on which the budget is based. These might be the growth rate of
certain indicators such as the GNP, possible government actions,
inflation rates, competitors' actions, or the possibility of strikes.
These assumptions should be discussed with top management so
that when the budget is submitted and accepted, both levels of
management have a complete understanding of the objectives
and risks.

On control of costs (one manager's ideas). In the construction
business, a most critical management responsibility is the control
of labor costs on each project. Our company has been reluctant
to go to "computerized," centralized cost reporting because of
the necessity for each project superintendent to be aware at all
times of his own labor costs (the only costs that he can control,
since purchasing is centralized). Therefore, we have placed the
responsibility for this reporting on the shoulders of the superintendent. Each day he prepares a diary, which indicates the items
of work performed and the raw labor cost for each item, coded
to the appropriate budget item. Weekly he prepares a cumulative
labor cost report directly from these diaries and indicates there-
on a comparison of the total costs to date with the budgeted
amount of each item and the quantities of work performed for
each item. Naturally, there is a certain amount of "fudging"
between individual cost items, but it is minimal, since the daily
report also shows the number of each labor craft employed, and

the total weekly labor costs must be reconciled with the payroll.

The greatest advantage to this system is the fact that the report is credible in the eyes of the superintendent. Furthermore, since the superintendent and management are intimately familiar with the costs, they are aware of potential problem areas as they arise and are prepared to act as necessary.

What about measurements and the young manager?

Measurements are one of the mechanisms by which organizations are controlled and they exist, in one form or another, in almost all companies. Unless the young manager deliberately sets out to discover what they are, he may go for too long a time without knowing how either he or his component is measured and who is doing the measuring. If he is working within a budget, of course, the budget figures are most important, but there may be many more measurements which are not explicitly stated and which may not be financial nor contained within the budget.

Having established which ones exist, the young manager can profitably start questioning the system. Why are those particular measurements used? How long have they been used? What are they really measuring? Are they the most significant which can be developed? Do they really measure the important elements? A very talented small device designer once told a group of engineering students an interesting story about how he worked. He said that when a design on which he may have been working for several months was finished, but before it was released for production, he again reviewed every dimension and asked himself the question, "Should this dimension be increased or could it be decreased? What are the implications if I change it in either direction?" This usually took several hours, but when the exercise was finished he was reasonably sure that he had not made any obvious mistakes and that he had a good reason for every dimension to be what it was. The young manager can follow a somewhat similar approach as he reviews the measurement system. Is it too elaborate or not elaborate enough? Is it too expensive for the results being obtained, or should more data be taken? These are the kinds of questions to be asked if he moves into a component which already has a system in operation. If, however, there is no system, then he has an open field to make a contribution. He can start at the beginning and develop one. As a guide, a class of questions similar to those found in Chapter 6 under planning can be developed, such as:

1. What are the objectives to be achieved by the work group?
2. What are the significant variables and resources?
3. What questions does the boss ask most often as to progress?
4. Can these points be covered by the measurements kept?

A young manager who analyzes and questions every measurement is certain to learn a great deal about the business in a hurry. If he can develop some new measurements which are more significant or responsive to the variables of the business, he can attract favorable attention. At the same time, however, he must be careful, for unfortunately some supervisors look on old-time measurements as sacred cows and their natural resistance to change has to be overcome—by tact and persuasion. Persuasion related to the manager's self-interest is potent.

Summary and some observations

1. Measurements are part of the control system and are accepted as essential.
2. It is more difficult to measure the professional worker than the factory worker.
3. People do best those things they are measured on, so if measurement is lacking, so is one type of motivation.
4. Profitability measurements are not enough.
5. Big companies tend to choke off initiative by too many measurements.
6. Most measurements are relative, not absolute.
7. Measurements which identify trends are often more important than absolute numbers.
8. It is essential that a business measure the performance of each functional area in a meaningful way.
9. Many measurements are unique to a kind of industry. Young managers should identify these and apply them to their own company if they are not being utilized.

10. Measurements must change because the business has a changing environment—both inside and outside the company.

11. New government regulations are of increasing importance, and businesses must develop new measurements to make sure they are in compliance.

12. Goals must be reasonable or they become self-defeating and no measurement system can compensate for them.

13. Alert young managers can make major contributions to their companies by analyzing needs and developing better measurements.

14. The relative importance of measurements changes with the times. For example, in periods of high money cost, inventory turnover is more important than when money cost is low.

The better the leader, the better the results.
The poorer the leader, the poorer the results.

The quality, the ability, the technique, the actuality of leadership is more highly prized by modern society and U.S. business than anything else except integrity.

The development of leadership qualities and the active exercise of leadership should be given high priority by young managers who aspire to more than average success as managers.

Paul M. Hammaker

It is often said that most people work well below their capacity. If a worker's self-motivation to work hard is low, then his production depends directly on the leadership qualities of his boss.

Louis T. Rader

8

Managing principle number six: Lead rather than drive your people

In days of great economic hardship, in times when jobs were scarce, in times when steady workers had only the bare necessities of life, many managers who were not leaders, who neither understood nor practiced the principles of leadership, were successful in production and even in selling. They had great economic power and their workers were fearful. Today such bosses would not even be hired—or if in the factory work force, would not be promoted to a managing position. Even very mediocre managers today are far closer to being leaders than the hard-boiled, seemingly heartless, intolerant, inflexible, "dammit, do it or get out" bosses of bygone days.

Young managers who want to achieve real success are well-advised to earn the followership of their people. Thus, instead of simply being an appointed boss, you—by virtue of what you are, what you do, and how you do it—become designated voluntarily by your people as their leader.

People would rather be led by a leader than bossed by a boss. Earning leadership at least in part depends on:

1. Understanding your people and their beliefs, goals, and frailties.

2. Creating sensible yet exciting or challenging goals.
3. Working in such a manner that you inspire your people to want to achieve the designated goals because this will give them satisfaction and a better life and help you and the company.
4. Acting confidently because you believe in yourself, your goals, and your people.
5. Being on the level, rewarding merit, and punishing sloth.
6. Creating a climate that enables your people to achieve for you and themselves the desired results.
7. When you have earned the confidence, respect, trust, and enthusiastic belief of your followers, you have the foundation for effective leadership.

Before discussing some of the qualities of leaders and leadership, we will give what we believe to be the basic test of a leader. The final test is the quality of performance turned in by the organization, both as individuals and as a team. Performance, good performance, is proof of the effectiveness of the leader.

All decisions and actions by the leader should be guided by his aim to secure superior performance. General Omar Bradley said he measured "the greatness of a leader by the achievements of the led."

We would have liked to offer a simple, accurate, comprehensive definition of a leader and leadership that would be particularly meaningful to young managers. We have discovered in this quest that while leaders and leadership are very real, they are also elusive. We have not succeeded in our attempt to put down in easy-to-understand language the essence and the spirit of leadership. Nor have we been able to find adequate definitions nor comprehensive descriptions of leaders. Skeats' *Etymological Dictionary of the English Language* in dealing with the word "lead" says it means "to show the way." Surely leaders do "show the way" to their people, so we find that definition OK as far as it goes.

A short and interesting definition of a good leader appeared in the *Time* magazine issue of July 15, 1974. Mortimer Adler, the philosopher, was quoted as saying:

. . . a good leader must have *ethos, pathos* and *logos.* The ethos is his moral character, the source of his ability to persuade. The *pathos* is his ability to touch feelings, to move people emotionally. The *logos* is his ability to give solid reasons for his action, to move people intellectually.

Many definitions or explanations of leaders and leadership are not very satisfying or else are a collection of such great qualities, such inspired actions, such noble orations that one wonders if any single human being ever was a leader if all the things spelled out are essential to leadership.

Despite the great problems in zeroing in on exactly what leaders are, what formed them, why they acted as they did, what lessons can they teach us, and similar matters, we ourselves (and we have observed it is true of many, many others also) are able to recognize leaders. How? By intuition, by gut feel, by insight? Suffice it to say that virtually every person we have ever talked with about leaders has without hesitation mentioned some. Perhaps they "just know."

Of course, all fields do have leaders, be they business, government, science, medicine, law, labor, religion. In fact, history in large measure is the story of the hopes, fears, successes, and failures of leaders. Our queries to young managers at this point are:

1. Who do you identify and recognize as leaders in your business? *Aom Rizza*
2. Who are leaders in your industry? *Issacs & Gilbert*
3. Who are leaders in U.S. business? *Aom. Rizza*
4. Who are some leaders in other fields that you are interested in such as pro football, civilian aviation, bowling, politics, boating, religion, education? *G. Parks, O. Alexgnder Brian Nordstrom*
5. Could you name some very great leaders who have had a significant impact on Western civilization? *Aom. Rizza*

We urge you to answer some or all of these questions. After you do, please specify the leaders you particularly admire and respect. Could they be models for you? If so, they become in a sense your personal leadership guides.

Also, analyze and identify for yourself the leaders you have

designated. What qualities did they have? *all good* What methods of
thinking did they follow? *The Admirals* How did they arrive at their objective
and settle on their mission? *The Admiral* How did they attract followers? *Money*
After they achieved leadership, how did they deal with their
followers? *Like shit.*

In an effort to be helpful to young managers, aspiring to
and/or engaged in the early stages of developing their leadership
ability, the authors offer the following observations:

1. You must have followers if you are to be a leader.
2. Leadership is rarely if ever bestowed on the leader. He has
   to earn it.
3. Leaders, though envied by many, do not have an easy life,
   but it is an interesting one.
4. To become a leader you have to pay a price. Part of the
   price is to struggle and arrive at great clarity of purpose.
   Another part is impose rather stern self-discipline. Another
   requirement is a feeling for people and a willingness to do
   the listening necessary to gain an understanding of what
   they are, and want, and desire to become.
5. The leader attracts followers. He has an appeal or appeals
   that make others want to become his followers. He gains
   acceptance, their acceptance. One appeal is that of a
   pleasing personality. Another appeal is that of competence.
   Still another appeal is the hope that the follower can learn
   from and be benefited by the leader. When an average
   Sunday-90 golfer finishes a round, no one follows him to
   his locker for advice and help. When Arnold Palmer goes to
   the locker room, he is often surrounded by men who are
   attracted to him because of his personality and competence
   as a golfer and they ask him for tips on how to cure a slice,
   how to get greater distance off the tees and many other
   matters. They hope to learn something and to improve their
   game. To the extent that Arnie is an effective teacher, he
   meets a leadership test: that is, improved performance by a
   student, a follower.
6. A good leader is a good teacher.
7. In addition to knowing, understanding and having real
   rapport with their people, leaders understand their business.

In this connection we analyzed a speech by an Army officer and found it relevant. As we get it, he said: "You can't fool your men. They know whether or not you know your business—and if you don't, you won't have their confidence." He believed an officer should know more about paper work than the company clerk, and more about food than the mess sergeant, and more about the problems of the troop's horses than the company farrier. He also added this: Where the officer couldn't excel, he ought to be as good as his best men. For example, he should be as good with the rifle as the best man in his company.

8. Leaders have a clear set of beliefs and values. In addition, they have a goal or objective or big appealing idea that they present frequently and persuasively to their followers. The objective can be as simple as to make the leader's particular section or department or division or region number one in a big company. It can be as simple as producing fewer seconds (imperfects) or making fewer billing errors or having lower bad debt losses this year than last year. Whatever it is, it must be of great importance to the leader and he must convince his people of its importance.

9. Leaders believe in themselves. They may appear humble or egotistical, but they all have great inner assurance. They are confident. That doesn't mean they are never discouraged, frustrated or almost at their wit's end. Despite trials and tribulations, they continue to believe in themselves, they are buoyed up by self-confidence.

10. Leaders, good ones, don't panic. Panic thinking is contagious. Avoid it!

11. Good leaders know that any order, or instruction, or decision that is quickly countermanded or drastically altered causes, at least, raised eyebrows. Followers expect a leader to know what he is doing and seldom, if ever, to cross himself up. When decisions have to be reversed, a full explanation, if it makes sense, helps the followers both to accept it and to maintain their confidence in the leader.

12. Leaders have courage. They have inner fortitude. They have guts. Their faith in whatever gods they have, their faith in themselves, their conviction as to the importance and

rightness of their mission all combine to sustain them in times of deep trouble and crisis. In such times, amazingly, they often present a calmness and confidence and expectancy of better times ahead that at least reassures and frequently inspires their followers.

13. Leaders believe in their people. They have confidence in them.

14. If a leader has managers reporting to him, a measure of the degree of confidence he has in them is shown by the amount of responsibility he delegates. Usually leaders delegate as much responsibility as they think the delegatee has the ability to assume and discharge.

15. A good leader knows that though he was delegated responsibility, along with the requisite authority, he, the leader, in the end is still responsible.

16. A good leader, though he delegates, does not abdicate. He must follow up, be informed, insist on his people being accountable. Accountability, at all levels in business, is a great discipline. Effectively used it is an insurance of responsible and effective behavior and actions.

17. A good leader keeps clearly in his mind and in the delegatee's minds that all decisions, wherever made, should be in tune with and assist the business to achieve its primary objectives.

18. Good leaders compile a good record as decision makers— even under conditions of great uncertainty. Such decisions in battle often face field officers. Our analysis of an Army officer's comments regarding this type of situation follows: In an emergency situation some officers keep their cool and give orders that are subsequently proven to be correct. Others appear to be in a blue funk. They give an order, revoke it, give another one, then change their minds again. Some would call the first type geniuses. They usually are not. However they have studied—they have visualized problems in advance—they have prepared themselves. Hence, they usually can cope with an emergency when they meet one. In an emergency or crisis, an officer must be able to think fast, identify the problem, decide what action to take, and order its execution. Any common-sense order is better than none.

The second type officer thinks—hunts—for an answer, decides, changes his mind, decides again, then changes his mind, and in the end does nothing. Enlisted men lack confidence in an officer who is a fuzzy thinker—who vacillates—who doesn't know his own mind. Enlisted men respect an officer who is calm, well-prepared, and decisive.

The first type officer if confronted by a situation he has never visualized nor imagined, will calmly reason as best he can. He is mentally disciplined and the chances are he will come up with some workable solution, give an appropriate order, and often win through. A field officer at times has to act without orders and if he has studied the thinking— work—decisions—actions of his superiors in the past, he has an idea of what his orders would be. Under these circumstances, the field officer can and usually does keep his cool and decides what to do relatively promptly. He is able to do so because as a student, a professional, a man who has grasped military strategy and tactics, he is prepared to deal with the unexpected on the basis of his self-confidence, mental power and ability to lead. The first type officer can be characterized as a leader-officer. He is superior to men who are only officers, just as leader-managers are better and get better results than men who are only managers.

19. A good leader knows that his people will do better work when they have earned by deeds not words his confidence, respect and trust, and hence he trusts them.

20. A good leader rewards merit and punishes sloth.

21. A leader knows he is a model to his people. This influences all aspects of his life.

22. Leaders rejoice in the growth and development of their people. They find ways to make their followers want to develop themselves.

23. Great leaders have infectious enthusiasm.

24. All great leaders are men/women of integrity. They are true to and dedicated to and pursue with great enthusiasm their objectives, or goal, or mission, or cause, or crusade.

25. Leaders never complete all the tasks they set for themselves. They do first things first. They do achieve much. Also they never finish selling, persuading, inspiring. They always find

new ground to plough, and new challenges for themselves and their followers.

The authors believe that sometimes most of us, and some people most of the time, learn the most about leadership and managing by looking at failures—by understanding the *don'ts*. The author of the following is unknown, but we think the author was a wise observer who had a keen eye and a sharp tongue. The title is "How Not to Be a Good Supervisor."

1. Never give your operators clear instructions ahead of time. Let them proceed on their own. Then, when they make mistakes, criticize them severely for any errors or omissions they may have made. Thus, you will be able to foster initiative and confidence.

2. Never commend a subordinate for a job well done, for this might spoil him. Kind words are not appropriate in a factory or office.

3. When criticisms, corrections, or reprimands are necessary, never administer them in private. Be sure that someone else is listening in on the procedure. It is better to have a large crowd so as to enhance your prestige.

4. Arrange to be busy with your own part of the work so that you cannot take time to help your operators on the job. You can best do this by not delegating work to those who are capable of doing it. This will force you to do most of the work yourself and will keep others from seeming to be as important as you are.

5. Never speak kindly to operators or subordinates or they will think that you are soft, or that you are a "good fellow." An honest-to-God supervisor should resemble Ivan the Terrible in dealing with his own force.

6. Avoid going over your mail for several days or even just let it stand unattended if you do look it over. This can conveniently be made to stretch out over weeks and more. The longer you take to approve a request or to respond to a communication from a subordinate, the more he will come to appreciate your importance.

7. If you don't understand or agree with what someone else is

trying to say, don't let him finish his arguments. Interrupt and cut him off at the third word of every sentence. After about the sixth or seventh time of this, he'll quit trying and you will find that you have then won your point—as a supervisor always should.

8. An excellent way to let your subordinate know that you have ideas of your own is to say to him, when you are considering a letter or report he has prepared, "Well, it's not the way I would have written it myself—but I'll sign it anyway." It also demonstrates your generosity and bigness of heart to say nothing of your broadminded willingness to overlook his minor faults!

9. Never waste any time training subordinates for possible advanced jobs. You won your way to your present supervisory position because you had an unusual combination of talent, concentration, and hard work. A helping hand is not appropriate in this "world of hard knocks."

10. Always remind your operators that their job is hanging on a thin thread, because it will keep them from too much confidence and security. The best way to keep people on their toes is to keep them on their knees.

Leadership involves many personal traits and though the "managing style" of business leaders varies, they all are able to command respect, and are supported by enthusiastic, convinced followers who believe in them. It is true that the followers execute the plans, do the work, and produce the profit, but the external motivating force to this body of people is the leader. He is apart from them in that he is the conceptualizer, the master persuader, their organizational peer, but is also an indispensable part of his vital and dynamic organization. He has a talent for wearing many hats. Two of them are the hat of the inspiring, goal-articulating leader. Another is that of the understanding, supportive member of his group who more than pulls his own weight.

Leadership involves being certain of your goals and exercising persistence, patience, and praise or the whip to motivate your people. Some leaders are clearly aggressive and others are more subtle. They keep a low profile but still relentlessly pursue, and see that their people pursue, clearly and rationally-defined and emotionally-described objectives.

All leaders we know of in business, whatever their manner, are keenly aware of the need for profit. They are attuned to change and devoted to getting improved results. They know, however, that waving a flag for dollar profit or a percent return on investment or the lowest unit cost or the smallest rate of seconds on returned goods is not enough. While such things are very important, they do not stir the pulses of men and women. Hence, the leader, knowing his people and their hopes, while keeping in mind his and the company's figure objectives, explains how the achievement of those objectives will produce rewards for and satisfactions to his people. His package of enticements and rewards includes increased recognition, higher status, more money, praise, sincere appreciation, and the ability and willingness to devote his complete attention to listening to his people individually, eye-to-eye, face-to-face. His recognition, whether a public acknowledgement of an individual's good work or a coveted invitation to dinner, fills the typical recipients with a warm glow of appreciation and satisfaction. If it doesn't, the leader is much less of a leader than he may think he is, or the recipient is walking down the profitless road of cynicism and negative thinking and is likely not a believer in the leader, and/or the company and its goals.

Business leaders do believe in themselves and they have the courage of their convictions. Thomas Paine, the author of *Common Sense,* the tract which influenced profoundly the shaping of Revolutionary America wrote,

I love the man who can smile in trouble, who can gather strength from distress and grow brave by reaction. 'Tis the business of little minds to shrink, but he whose heart is firm, and whose conscience approves his conduct, will pursue his principles to death.

Business leaders are "take charge" men or women. They tend to be—almost without exception—decisive. They are not wishy-washy. They don't flood their talk with disclaimers, nor are they vague and obscure.

Business leaders earn and deserve high marks for their ability to communicate. We don't mean merely that they talk. We do mean that they have a grasp of their people, their business, their competitors, the world around them. What they say both makes sense and is tailored in content, language, and tone to their audience. Though the message is essentially the same, their communications—always on the level—differ greatly between a talk with a dozen plant foremen and a dozen polished, sophisticated financial analysts. To put it bluntly, they know to whom they are talking and what to say. They know what they are talking about.

Business leaders are, by necessity, possessed of great skill in the art of persuasion. Because they know, if not love, people, they recognize that their people want to see the company succeed and also make all the money they can as individuals as well as gain a lot of individual, personal self-satisfaction. They recognize the necessity of persuading their people, that the interests of the company and the individual are compatible—and they persuade.

Leaders in business are people-oriented; they are also people sensitive.

Is a young manager a business leader? He is not in the sense that the head of General Motors, AT&T, or U.S. Steel is. Nonetheless, assuming similar ability and competence, the more successful managers at all levels are leaders. They practice the art of leadership. The leader of a great corporation wasn't born into that position. He achieved it by exercising leadership at many other positions, in many other responsibilities as he earned promotions and successively higher positions.

We believe that leadership can be developed. While there are some "natural" leaders due to their personality, character, and natural physical and other endowments, there are a multitude of managers—leaders at all levels in U.S. business—who achieved the leader-manager position by intelligently working at their personal growth and development as an individual first and as a businessman second.

If a young manager desires to develop leadership qualities—and, indeed, become a leader-manager—he can do such things as discover:

1. Does anyone look at him as being a leader?
2. If so, what do they see in him?

3. If so, do they think he lacks or is weak in certain ways?
4. If so, what are they?
5. Does he agree?
6. If so, does he want to change his weaknesses into strength?
7. If so, what does he need to do?
8. If he can't figure it out, who does he trust and can talk to about himself with the likelihood of getting help?
9. If nobody, what can he read that will be useful?

Whether the above steps are followed or not, if no one thinks he is a leader, can he become one?

The authors think—given that the young manager has demonstrated enough brains, ability, and wisdom to have been made a manager—that he can through study, observation, and self-analysis develop the wit to lay out a self-improvement course that will enable him to evolve into a leader-manager. This is likely to lead him to, among other things, the study of leaders and leadership. The bookshelves are full of self-help books. A very good one is Dale Carnegie's, *How to Stop Worrying and Start Living.* Also, thousands of managers have developed poise and communication skills through Carnegie's public speaking courses, and many hundreds of them have thus enhanced their leadership potential. In this secular age you may chuckle when we say and believe that most any open-minded young manager can enhance his leadership potential greatly by reading, studying, digesting, understanding the world's all time best seller, the Bible. There are many versions available. Of course another great source of help in the development of one's personality and leadership potential is Shakespeare, as well as the biographies of great men. In another area are the educational courses dealing with managerial improvement offered by various associations such as the American Management Association seminars and schools such as the University of Virginia Graduate School of Business Administration. These range from one-day briefings to the six weeks' executive programs.

There is no dearth of available material for a manager who wants to become a leader-manager. Those desiring to make this happen need only lay out a program for individual growth and development and follow it. Such action—done well and with persistence—can pay big dividends in money and personal satisfaction.

In some way, all business managers assist directly—
or indirectly—by their actions to produce a profit or
a loss. If you believe profits are ethically or morally
wrong, you should get out of business, because if
you don't believe in the need for and rightness of
profits, you likely will hurt rather than help the
business that pays your salary. And, equally important, you will be prostituting a basic conviction of
yours—thus destroying to some extent your personal
integrity.

Paul M. Hammaker

The universal and final measurement in business is
profit. Any bum off the street can run a business at
a loss.

Louis T. Rader

9

Managing principle number seven: Earn a profit

The necessity of profit applies to all commercial enterprises that want to survive over time. Amplified, managing principle number seven is: Manage so that customers are pleased enough with your company's products and/or services that they give you, instead of your competitors, enough sales at prices to more than cover all your costs and, thereby, enable your business to *earn a profit.*

Every commercial business must be profitable in order to enable it to continue to pay dividend wages to the stockholders, salary wages to the workers, and, in general, to bolster the U.S. economy and benefit our society.

Previous chapters have dealt with six managing principles. These management principles are expected to enable the manager, whether in a huge multinational corporation or a medium-size or small company, to meet a primary mission—namely, to earn profits. It should be clearly understood that even though all six of these managing principles are applied, if the business does not make profits it is headed for trouble—even for failure and bankruptcy.

Jobs are created by the investment of capital. Capital represents accumulated savings. Savers want interest or dividends or some kind of a return on their money. Most stockholders who invest their funds in a business want dividends. Banks and insurance companies who loan money to business for short-term and long-term periods want interest. In addition, some financial institutions when approached by an entrepreneur for money not only want interest but they also want a piece of the action. That is, they want some stock, some equity in the enterprise.

The alternative to providing capital for business from private sources is to have government-owned and operated businesses who secure their capital by taxation directly and/or indirectly and/or by deficit financing or by some other device which extracts from some or all citizens the funds necessary to build, say, a steel mill. Typically, this is the situation which exists in Russia. Capital has got to come from somewhere, but in this country we have elected for 200 years as a nation to say that most of our economic activity will be private enterprise and that capital will be provided by private not public sources.

Profit is not only essential to attract capital which in turn provides jobs, but it also is a measure of relative competence. When all things are approximately equal and when a half dozen businesses in the same field have after-tax profits that range from 2 percent to 8 percent, it is quite clear that from the viewpoint of owners, lenders, investors, financial analysts, and many others that the company earning 8 percent demonstrates greater managerial competence than do the 2 percent performers.

Without pursuing the subject of profit any further, suffice it to say that one of the missions of private enterprise is to earn a profit. In the authors' opinion the six managing principles mentioned earlier can produce a profit when coupled with the production and sale of a desired product or the offering and delivery of a desired service. Private companies, however nobly inspired, however socially responsible, however ethically sensitive, however humane, or paternalistic or socially-oriented, must never lose sight of one aspect of their primary mission, which is to earn a profit. The other aspect of their primary mission is to provide desired goods and/or services. The first part of the mission is what attracts investors. The second part is what attracts customers. When both investors and customers are satisfied, there is always a profit.

The profit responsibility of every individual in a business exists, though to many it is quite unclear. So far as his function is concerned, the worker on an assembly line at General Motors must perform productively and well compared with the production worker at Ford, Chrysler, American Motors, Volkswagen, Mercedes Benz, Volvo, Saab, and Fiat. If the General Motors production worker produces his part of the product which is noticeably unsatisfactory in quality, or produces his portions of the product at a cost that is noticeably too high related to competition, then he as one individual performing a needed function is working in a way that is injurious to profit. The actions of one worker will not determine the final profit results. However, if many workers fail to discharge their profit responsibility, then the company's results will be sharply, adversely affected.

The same points apply to foremen, and all of the ranks of management, whether they be specified as lower management, middle management, senior management, or top management. Manufacturing managers may say that "All I have to do to discharge my profit responsibility is to produce a good product at a fair cost." A sales manager may say, "All I have to do is to sell enough product at a fair price to keep the factories busy." Someone, and this is the general manager or chief executive officer's responsibility, has to see that the total of all costs incurred—be they research and development, engineering, manufacturing, sales promotion, advertising, personnel administration, legal, control and accounting, or whatever—are less than the selling price. Whatever is left is pretax profits. In most corporations, the U.S. government via its corporate income tax has declared itself to be about a 50 percent partner. In other words, about one half of pretax profits are paid to the government. The amount then remaining is net profit and that is the sum out of which wages for money saved and invested into the business are paid via dividends to stockholders, and out of that sum come various kinds of capital and other expenditures by the business that are a major source of new jobs.

The foregoing is a simple, accurate portrayal of the basic economics of private enterprise. Unfortunately, they are not well known. Unfortunately, many discussions—particularly in social and political areas—take place without a recognition of the basics just mentioned.

What has all this to do with the young manager? It is one of the authors' basic beliefs that the more the young manager knows about his business and about his industry and about business in general, the better off he will be. It is particularly important for young managers who aspire to grow and achieve increasingly responsible and increasingly well-compensated positions to understand their business, their industry, the business system and, indeed, all of the elements external to a business which have an impact on that business.

The young manager may have observed—as have the authors—that except in rare instances, internal costs and costs for goods and/or services purchased outside go up—seldom down. This makes cost improvement and cost avoidance a continuing challenge facing almost all managers. Coming up with the ideas and methods for controlling and/or reducing costs are usually a means that young managers can use to gain recognition and advancement.

Profit is made in various ways and many companies have a definite commitment to one way or the other. Some concentrate on new technology in their product, some on low selling price, some on unusual features or attributes, some on the full market-basket approach, and so on. These approaches are contained within the general term "corporate strategy" and must involve an integration of the tasks of each functional area of the business. But whatever the strategy, a company must at least be as efficient as competitors to survive, and this is what has forced the study of all aspects of operations—aspects such as organization structure, planning, measurement, integration and control. These many approaches to efficiency tend often to mask the fundamental raison d'etre of a company, that of being profitable, and it was the need to emphasize this over and over again that led to Rader's Rules (discussed in Chapter 2). It is rather amazing, but quite reassuring, how often seemingly complicated problems can be resolved by a simple statement, if the statement is quite fundamental. A good example of this is the following.

For all his properly great reputation for financial acumen, Hal Geneen of IT&T was most receptive to very simple arguments if they told a story. In one case, he was trying to dissuade one of his men from taking a job as president with another company. Hal pointed out all the problems in the other company, the fact that they were losing $25 million on $250 million sales, the deterioration of morale that must exist, the lack of good planning, and so on. The middle manager, wanting to leave with Geneen's good will and respect, said, "Hal, you've always told us that the fundamental rule for running a business is to spend less than comes in. Now this company brings in $250 million and this figure is pretty firm, but they spend $275 million, so my job as I see it would be to cut the spending down below $250 million, and I think I can do it." Wherewith Geneen had to smile and was grudgingly satisfied.

Managers are given credit only for results, not for the intensity of effort expended. How does one achieve results? There are so many variables in the running of a business that it is well-nigh impossible to tabulate all the things which a manager must do correctly in order to be effective. With the thought that it might be more useful to identify the factors which tend to cause failure, one of the authors after many years of observation, compiled the following list. These we have labeled "Cardinal Sins of Management."

On some cardinal sins of management

1. Thinking that if you work very hard you shouldn't be held responsible for nonrealization of overall goals.
2. Believing you should be promoted when you have not developed a successor.
3. Believing that a good system—paperwork or computer management information system—is all you need to get results; and is more important than people performance.
4. Believing that good breaks (luck, fortune) in products, the economy, misfortunes of your competitors are your due, but that you are not expected to overcome bad breaks.
5. Refusing to take responsibility for mistakes or nonperformance of subordinates.
6. Believing that you know more than the customer about what he wants.

7. Believing that if you *do everything* suggested by your boss, or the employee relations manager, or by the rule book but don't get results, you are off the hook.

8. Believing that your problems are more complex—for whatever reason—than are your competitors'.

9. Believing that a happy and contented work force is incompatible with high standards of performance.

10. Believing that major problems should be kept from the boss as long as possible.

11. Believing that your employees cannot really understand the necessity for competitive skill, care, and effort or the need for quality or meeting promised shipping dates.

12. Believing there will be no major problems of a new kind arising in the coming year.

13. Believing that employees will do their best work if there is no measurement of it.

14. Delegating all planning responsibility to the planners and letting them make major decisions.

15. Believing that U.S. methods of running a business are the best which can be used in any country.

16. Believing that people behave logically.

17. Believing that a manager should only pay attention to big things and not bother with details: Details such as:

    a. cleanliness in a factory
    b. absenteeism or tardiness
    c. usage of a computer

18. Blaming all problems on a lack of communication.

The authors' advice to young managers is to make sure of the following:

1. Know the basic economic facts of life.
2. Recognize and approve the importance of profits.
3. Determine—irrespective of whether you're in sales, manufacturing, accounting, or whatnot—what relationship your operation has to the profits of the business.
4. Determine what kinds of actions in the sphere of your responsibility could add to profit; have neither favorable nor unfavorable impact on profits; have an unfavorable impact on profit.

5. Come up with ideas or changes which will benefit profits.
6. Recognize that profits is more than a number; that it is the result of a host of activities well performed related to competition, along with the offering and sale of goods or services that enough customers prefer to those offered by your competitors so that you can at the end of a year and at the end of the income statement, have a satisfactory profit.

A simple, sound, easy-to-read explanation of basic economics and the importance of profit can be found in a small inexpensive book, *How We Live,* published by the American Economic Foundation, 51 E. 42nd Street, New York, N.Y.

I think it is harder to be an outstanding manager in a nonprofit institution than in a business that must earn profits in order to survive.

The first six managing principles in this book can be applied to nonprofit institutions to the ultimate benefit of all concerned.

Paul M. Hammaker

Too many people imply that because they work for a nonprofit organization they do not have to be efficient in a measurable sense and object even to making a search for a measurement of productivity. But even nonprofit organizations must have money to operate and an attitude of indifference to measurement threatens their whole existence.

The absence of competition is the main reason why so many nonprofit organizations could equally correctly be called nonefficient organizations.

Louis T. Rader

10

Management principles in nonprofit organizations

The nonprofit organizations in this country account for a large percentage of the gross national product and employ a large percentage of all workers. The major ones are government—federal, state, and municipal; education—kindergarten through college—and hospitals and related health care services. In addition, there are many other lesser categories, such as foundations, economic and social and political research, and educational; professional societies, trade associations which exist to interchange information; cultural such as, art museums, ballet, symphony.

The question often arises as to whether business principles which apply to profit and loss (P&L) organizations can be applied to this not-for-profit category. There are many who believe they cannot be applied, and others who feel no attempt should even be made. One of the authors was in a university meeting once when a department chairman stated that the words "cost-effectiveness" and "education" should not be used in the same sentence. Even the simplest analysis points out major differences which exist between the profit and not-for-profit organizations and which perhaps give rise to the feeling that there is no basis for application. Some of these differences—

not always applicable to all situations—are the following:

In the P&L sector, competitors always exist. Resistance to change or risk taking is inherent in any organization of any complexity. If in a P&L company a component says something cannot be done, someone in the organization has to ask the question, "Are we sure enough that it cannot be done that we are willing to bet no competitor will do it? And, if he does, will we then lose position in the category being discussed?"

This throws many judgments into a relative rather than absolute phase. To maintain we can't do it is one thing, but to maintain that no competitor can or will do it is something else again.

This is part of the discipline of competition or of the market place. Nonprofit organizations are not faced with this. There is no competition for a local school system or for a municipal hospital, or for the state government. Anyone in those organizations can say, "It can't be done," and there is presumably little recourse on the part of the manager who may want it done. The absence of well-defined competition is then a major point of difference.

A second major difference is the existence of objectives, written or understood. The principal objective of a P&L business can be stated many ways, but everyone knows that to exist it must stay solvent, not go broke, and make some money over a period of time. There is no comparable universal measurement in the not-for-profit organization. P&L businesses, by and large, develop other objectives to go with the profit one. These may be growth rates, share of the market, new fields and products to go into, productivity improvements, geographical dispersion including overseas markets, or whatever. But they know, or believe, that objectives written and disseminated through the organization constitute a strong motivating force around which the organization can plan and execute. The not-for-profit organizations rarely have such written objectives. In a school system, for instance, the superintendent of schools seldom enunciates what the school objectives are with regard to handling talented or retarded children, and special teachers for music, art, or remedial reading. He knows what the right answer is for excellent education, but he is also constrained by the school board's budget. The latter organization, in turn, is presumably responsive to the community's wishes, but what are those wishes? Unless some organization like the PTA takes the initiative to ask the right questions, and consolidate community thinking into a set of objectives which can be translated into suggestions to the school board, little may be done. The problem is a serious one. In a book published some years ago by the Fund for the Advancement of Education, the author, Paul Woodring, stated that the philosophy of education must come from the people, although the people find it very difficult to verbalize them.

The problems of the delivery of the health care industry are still more serious because of the various populations they serve. The school serves the parents of school-age children, which is a well-defined population, though all taxpayers carry the cost. The hospital, on the other hand, must be responsive to all the people of the community. It must be responsive to federal, state, and municipal regulations. It must have defined policies for the training of nurses, interns, and paramedicals. So what are its objectives? Can they be verbalized?

A third significant difference between the two major categories of profit and nonprofit organizations is the area over which the service offered extends, or may extend. There are no restrictions on the field of activity of a P&L company. It can operate in any state it chooses, subject to relevant state laws. It can discontinue operations in one part of the country and re-start in another. The nonprofits identified as major above do not have this freedom. For example, a municipal hospital or school is viable only in its own community. It has no meaning outside it. Accordingly, it must live with all the problems which occur in that community. It is meaningless to talk of closing up and starting somewhere else.

The problem of people motivation in a not-for-profit organization is serious primarily because of the absence of competition. Appeals can be made to performance within budget, but too many know that the setting of such budgets is often within the realm of gamesmanship—that is, to ask for as much as possible in the hopes of getting some major fraction of it. Also, position levels are unfortunately often proportional to monies spent rather than to accomplishments.

In view of all this, then, can business managing principles 1 through 6 which are effective in P&L organizations be applied to nonprofit organizations? We believe they can and should be, even though the problems are more difficult.

The objectives of the organization can be identified. Operating people can and should ask their school board, or hospital board, or even city council what the objectives are or should be. These can then be written down and modified as new thinking develops.

Planning for the future can and should be done. Even if there is no way by which growth rates can be estimated for the next three to five years, projections can be made for all three possible cases—a decline in growth, a level situation, and an increase. The projections can include an analysis of people requirements and capital investments.

In the absence of profitability as such, an alert manager in nonprofit organizations can get ratios on the operation of other organizations similar to his own. The cost of a hospital bed per day is a significant number. If, in addition, it is corrected for prevailing labor rates, energy rates, material cost, it is a minimum starting point for examining cost-effectiveness. The same is true for expenditures per pupil per year—again with caution to make sure the comparison is meaningful. We believe it is safe to say that comparative measurements can be obtained and can be useful for almost any phase of the organization's activity.

The many special personnel practices which exist in nonprofit organizations (such as tenure in education, and civil service regulations in government) may make the motivating of people to continuously expend good, intelligent effort a more serious problem than in P&L companies. Good leadership, despite the frustrations which bureaucracy may engender, is still a powerful force if exercised.

What about not-for-profit organizations and young managers?

There are many opportunities to apply sound business principles to the management of nonprofit organizations. The opportunity is the greater because so many believe little can be done.

Meaningful measurements can be discovered or developed. Means for motivating people can also be found. Planning can be done. The term "cost-effectiveness" can be used in the same sentence with "education," "hospital" or "government."

There is no doubt in the authors' minds that managing principles one through six can be successfully and usefully applied by managers, both young and mature, in not-for-profit institutions.

The desire to assist and influence your boss in subtle and direct ways by enabling him to concentrate on matters where he is especially able and competent while you supplement him in his areas of weakness makes him, the company, and you all winners. All winners and no losers is a delightful combination and you may be able to make it happen. It isn't easy but many managers do it.

Paul M. Hammaker

It's a great mistake to think a boss got where he is by accident and that he is not really bright or competent. And a worse mistake is to share this thought with your wife or husband.

Louis T. Rader

11

On managing yourself and your boss

If this chapter were titled "How to Manage Your Boss," it would be newsworthy—just as is the famous headline—"Man Bites Dog." Traditional wisdom says bosses manage the people reporting to them.

One statement made about bosses is that they achieve their goals and accomplish their results through the work of others. If you as a manager can arrange matters so that your boss advances your cause and helps you achieve the results desired by you and/or required from you, then in this sense are you managing your boss? Are you *his* manager to some degree? Perhaps it is a two-way street where each of you do some managing of the other.

We know bosses have to depend on their people. We know those managers reporting to a boss are dependent on him for promotion, salary increases, work satisfaction, and, hence, to some considerable extent, for the quality of their lives. Actually the boss and the managers reporting to him are mutually dependent—as well as being—in some degree mutual bosses.

If you aspire to "manage your boss" there are a number of things to consider.

1. To be successful at this, know what it really means to help your boss. It means to be of great value to him because your work clearly advances his—and the company's—interests.
2. Your boss like almost all other managers has strong and weak points. He would rather do certain things (such as talk with people) than other things (such as digest reports).
3. If you can help him with the tasks he finds less pleasant or even distasteful, then he can spend more time on the things he likes best. It is likely that he does best the things he likes best. If he spends more time on what he does best, the chances are results will be better. This will benefit him and the company.
4. In order to make this possible a young manager must establish a good relationship with his boss. He must have or gain a good understanding of his boss.

So if such an interest exists, a good starting point is to ponder and discover what is your boss's interest in you. What does he want from you? Bosses come in all sizes and shapes. They have a wide range of ideas. As long as you are working for a specific boss his ideas—whatever they are—are important to you.

The least almost any boss will be interested in is that you perform up to his standards whatever they may be. To be utterly simplistic (and that's not all bad), your boss wants you to do your work well and to be a satisfactory employee.

It is up to you to fill in what that means.

A good many bosses want their people to be at work every day, to be at work on time, be willing when necessary to work long hours, to do their particular work efficiently, to keep them informed so there are no unpleasant surprises. Different bosses have different ideas, such as: do what you're told, *or* exercise initiative; be a planner, *or* I'll do the planning around here; make suggestions, *or* don't rock the boat; train your people, *or* they know more than you do; accept them as they are, *or* let them teach you; create team spirit, *or* if everybody does their work we won't need to worry about team spirit; become ready to succeed him, *or* (not stated but clearly signaled) don't become a threat to my job security; move around the company a little and get favorably known, *or* you work in this department, you stay in this department, you better be too busy to go making friends in other departments.

If you've had several bosses what were they interested in?

Since your present boss has a lot to do with your business success, how can you find out what he desires and treasures and rewards, and what he ignores or dislikes or puts a low value on and what kind of thinking and acting he punishes? This is a key question.

You can learn these things by considering and evaluating:

1. What he tells you.
2. What others tell you about him.
3. What he does, his actions.
4. Do his words and actions agree?
5. What does he reward?
6. What does he in fact *punish* by withholding promotion, no pay increase, putting men on probation, moving men to a dead-end job, firing?

In your own particular situation, you as a manager analyzing your boss may decide there are additional factors to consider.

Now to shift gears—what are some things you want in a boss? Your simplistic reply could be: I want a boss on the move upward who will help me to become good enough so I can succeed him.

In your specific situation you may decide you want to alter, amplify, delete, or improve on this! If so, the authors suggest it is a good idea to write down your thoughts. In any event it is up to you to fill in some details. Do you want your boss to be rational, fair, demanding, one who acknowledges achievements, one who gives you leeway, one who will not beat you to death for making a mistake, a planner, a man who pays his people as well as they deserve and the company permits, a man of integrity, a leader, a man who'll be promoted, a boss who will recommend that you succeed him when he moves up, *if* you deserve to?

Now let's suppose your boss is a good deal less than the ideal you have defined. What are the possibilities related to his future actions—as a boss?

They are: he'll stay unchanged; he'll improve in your view;

he'll retrogress in your view. Maybe you'll be able to accept some of his deficiencies and even get a chuckle out of them. A friend of ours was an assistant to the president of a large store. The president was so flexible he was mercurial. Our friend, after establishing rapport with his boss, would go to the president's office each morning, salute and smilingly, ask: "What is our policy today? High sales and low markup? *Or* high markup and low sales?"

Now we come to a question that you may answer. (We have, at least, to our own satisfaction.) Can you have an effect on your boss that will enable him to do a better job?

You certainly cannot *if* it's not worth the time and trouble, by study and analysis and common sense, to *understand* him, and then by conscious planned effort to build a special relationship with him.

What are some things—basic—to building a special relationship wherein he comes to treasure you and you to appreciate him? They include:

1. Loyalty.
2. Dependability.
3. Doing a superior job that reflects credit on him.
4. Listening to him and trying on his problems for size.
5. Having ideas, alternatives, new ways to do things that are better.
6. A genuine belief in the boss as a manager and as a man (he isn't perfect, but don't you believe his strengths outweigh his weaknesses?).
7. Personal rapport.

If you really can't do these things, you need a new boss or an improved model of *you.*

If you aspire to help your boss by changing him in important ways, remember that this is a long row to hoe and a dangerous one. Why not "accept him as he is and build the initial part of your career around making him look good." The better the boss performs (if you really helped him), the better you are in his eyes.

We assume that you will establish rapport with your boss and earn his confidence and respect based on your actions and your character. Also we assume you will or have come to respect your boss for his character and ability and performance.

If you aspire to manage him or influence him constructively to a significant degree, for his benefit and yours, it is essential that you understand him. Understanding revolves around an appreciation of what manner of man he is—what are his ambitions, goals, and personal values—and what makes him tick. A possible further approach to lead you to a good understanding of your boss is that presented by the philosopher Eduard Spranger, who identified six kinds of value orientation. Spranger wrote of theoretical man, economic man, aesthetic man, social man, political man, and religious man.[1] Most men have all such values, but usually one or two are predominate. Spranger uses these six words—*theoretical, economic, aesthetic, social, political,* and *religious* in the following way:

Theoretical Man—a searcher after truth. He observes, reasons, is rational and is a scientific type.

Economic Man—is attuned to what is useful. He is practical, interested in production and marketing and in acquiring personal wealth. He often is a businessman—though not all successful businessmen have the economic as their predominate interest.

Aesthetic Man—is interested in art, in form, grace, symmetry. He often is not an artist but does appreciate, and places a high value on, beauty.

Social Man—loves people. He is often unselfish, kind, and generous. He usually regards love as the key to good human relationships.

Political Man—prizes, works for, and often achieves power. He tends to be quite competitive. Most leaders are strongly power-oriented. He is likely to be a businessman or a politician.

Religious Man—is keenly interested in the highest and finest things and values. He may be a bit mystical. He seeks to relate to the universe—to the eternal verities. He tries to create ideal situations.

Another way of looking at bosses is to see if they are oriented as Blake and Moulton (discussed in Chapter 3) express it—to

---

[1] William D. Guth and Renato Tagiuri, "Personal Values and Corporate Strategies," *Harvard Business Review,* September-October 1965.

people or to production or both. They believe that many bosses are interested in production—not people—*or* are interested in people and care little about production, though there are managers who have a high regard for high production and for the welfare and development of their people.

If you find merit in the ideas of the authors or those of Spranger or Blake and Moulton in sizing up and understanding your boss—good. If not, and you wish to progress and be extremely useful to your boss, then you need to develop for yourself ways to arrive at a comprehensive and generally accurate understanding of him.

Assuming you have a good understanding of your manager and have established a good working and personal relationship, let us explore briefly ways in which you can help him above and beyond what may be called for in your job description. For instance:

1. If he hates to write reports and his reports are poor ones and you are good at writing reports you have a great opportunity to help him. If you have built a good relationship, you can give him report drafts. He uses them as he sees fit. Chances are his reports will be better.

2. If he hates to read reports but likes to talk with people in his office and in the field and you are good at reading, digesting, and summarizing reports, then you have a real opportunity to help him. If you have built a good relationship, soon you can give him report digests and summaries, thereby using your strength to compensate for his weakness.

3. If he doesn't have many ideas but when he hears a good one he buys it, this offers you an opportunity. You can dream up and search out ideas. You can give them to him and help him develop and make reality out of them.

4. If he is a great motivator of people but not a great problem solver this can be an opportunity you can help him with. Some problems which are at a higher level than you are likely to encounter in your initial job, but will have to face early in a retail career are how to sell up from lower-quality and price items to higher-quality and price ones; how to improve margin; how to serve customers better; how to improve profit.

So in your own interest, and to supplement your boss's weakness and to benefit the company, you become a problem solver—and let your boss take the credit if he desires to do so. Of course, it will be beneficial to you if the boss depends on you to a considerable extent to be his problem solver.

Problem solving requires a skill, a method and a good deal of hard work. The primer approach that is both simplistic and valid is:

State the problem! What is the problem? Is it poor profit? No. Profit is a result not a cause. Identifying the causes of a problem enables you to state the problem in stark terms that represent the battleground where the fight must be won if the problem is to be solved.

If the problem is a basic one which must be addressed by senior and middle management, then in your early career you won't have to deal with it. However, after a promotion or two you will.

Let's say the problem is defined as: "Inability to compete in quality, price, delivery, and customer service due to our top management's obsolete concepts and strategy with corresponding failure on the part of our top engineering, manufacturing, marketing, and financial people." Is that a good problem statement? No. It is only the start of a good statement; it is tactless, general, and too all-embracing. It both ignores corporate strengths and fails to identify carefully and specifically what smaller areas—what groups and what specific policies and practices—do really represent the problem.

So more study and analysis is necessary. This should lead to a statement of the problem. Such a statement could be: "Our company's competitive quality, price, service policy permits charging higher prices than our competitors' do. This policy is being used by a major competitor to their sales advantage and our sales disadvantage. Our lowered sales are a cause of our declining profit."

The policy which is now in effect and is currently a reason for the poor sales and profit performance says: "We will be generally competitive considering company reputation, brand acceptance, market share, company profitability, the range of competitive specifications, relatively fail-free performances, on-time delivery, and generous adjustment policy by pricing our goods within a range of not more than 10 percent above competition nor 15 percent below it. We believe our reputation for quality is unmatched by our competitors—and at times—permits us to charge a somewhat higher price."

Once the problem is well defined and stated, the question arises: What can be done to solve it? There are possible and differing answers—alternatives. In this case, several different proposed revised policy statements should be prepared—each of which could overcome the basic current difficulty. Thus, several alternatives worth considering are stated. Spell out and present the good and bad aspects of each alternative.

Arrive at a conclusion and recommendation—supported by available evidence and pertinent reasoning. In addition to the advantages of the recommended policy change with the intended corrective action, point out the risks involved. Also, if possible, be prepared to discuss what can and should be done *if* the proposed action fails.

5. If your boss does not have an early-warning system on problems that are likely to arise and you develop sources of information and a feel for possible future problems, this is a great opportunity for you. You can become a kind of sensitive antenna zeroed in on possible future difficulties. As you become aware of what may prove to be unfavorable developments, you can—if you have real rapport with your boss—lay your thoughts concerning them before him.

This does not mean carrying gossip to your boss—or tales of woe or vague generalities. Not only are such things usually of little or no value, but bringing them to your manager may lead to a situation where he doesn't want to see you or hear from you.

To recap: If you want to help your boss—some areas where you may be able to do so, depending on such factors as those covered earlier are: writing report drafts for him, summarizing reports for him, providing him with ideas, problem solving, anticipating problems or possible future problems.

If you, as a manager who knows his own job—who understands his boss—who identifies areas where you can be especially useful to the boss—and you do these things—are you helping your boss? Yes. Is the boss therefore getting better results? Yes.

Is getting results through others managing? Yes. Are you under the circumstances outlined, therefore, to some degree managing your boss? Yes. Is this good? We think so.

We think it is good because the company, your boss and you are all winners—when you constructively and subtly manage—or at least influence—your boss in the ways suggested here, or in many other ways that specific managers have discovered and used. In fact, the kind of situation we have described is ideal— because it is all profit—and no loss, for all concerned.

Query: Should I as a manager attempt to the full extent of my ability to understand, undergird, help my boss?

Answer: Yes.

Query: Do I have to say—even to myself—that this as discussed in this chapter amounts to managing my boss, at least to some extent?

Answer: No—you don't: In fact, it's better not to think about it in such a way—even though it may be a fairly accurate statement.

Query: Is building rapport with the boss, becoming his good right arm and influencing him in constructive ways acting politically, unethically, and being underhanded?

Answer: If you act out of sincerity, with integrity, and are working for your boss's best interest—and the company's too— this is desired and ethical behavior.

Nothing is more disastrous for a young manager than to adopt a "superior," patronizing manner designed to inflate his ego, and to believe he is smarter than his boss and to tell all and sundry that he does manage his boss.

We recommend building great rapport with your boss— planning, talking, acting in your boss's and therefore the company's best interest. It's OK to become a star team player—but don't blow your own horn. Let your boss (if he believes it—and it is true) tell others how good and helpful and constructive your actions are.

You can, to a great degree, manage your career
and hence your business future. Beyond that, you
can plan for and achieve a full and rewarding total
life. Business success, as you define it, is important.
Success in your family, community, church, and
social life is important, too. The challenge is to
arrive at a program and action plan that makes your
total life satisfying—then to make it happen.

Paul M. Hammaker

If you don't do any planning of your own career,
it will be done for you by others—your parents,
your spouse, and later even your children. All at
once it may dawn on you that you are not living
the life you really wanted to live.

Louis T. Rader

I know of no more encouraging fact than the
unquestioned ability of man to elevate his life by
conscientious endeavor. If one advances confidently
in the direction of his dreams, and endeavors to live
the life he has imagined, he will meet with a success
unexpected in common hours.

Henry David Thoreau

12

On managing your future and career planning

One of the requirements in the second year of the Graduate School of Business at the University of Virginia is a paper on career planning. Some of the students have told us that it was the most valuable assignment they had had in the two years because it forced them to make a road map of their future.

Someone once said, "If you don't know where you are going, any road will get you there"—and, it might be added, you don't even know if you have arrived at where you would like to be if you didn't know where you were going in the first place.

All the organizations that teach management principles— whether General Electric, the American Management Association, or business schools—include planning as a major area. Nearly everyone in business believes in planning of some sort. But despite this agreement as to what is good for a business, most business and professional people do very little planning for their own personal life. This lack of planning is not confined to young people. Even men and women in their 40s and 50s often wake up to the fact that they are unhappy or vaguely dissatisfied with their life, whether they are in industry, government, or in universities.

Not long ago in a discussion a professor said to a friend, "I'm unhappy. I'm just 39 years old. I'm a full professor. I have a national reputation in my field. But I don't know where I'm going." So the friend asked, "Where do you want to go? Do you want to be a department head or a dean or a college president? Or do you want to try your skills in industry or government? Would any of these jobs make you happier? Or have you ever thought this specifically about it?" The young professor replied, "Those are good questions. I guess I don't know what I want and I'd better start thinking about it." So, because he was a friend, the other said, "You know you have no right to say you are unhappy unless you can say why—whether it's location, geography, money, or whatever. But more important, you should discover and identify what it would take to make you happy."

Self-analysis

A career does not have to be a completely haphazard affair, even though everyone recognizes that chance, or luck, will always be in the picture. A first step in career planning is to do a little self-analysis and at least decide what you want. A possible broad objective, for any of us, is to be happy. Too many make the assumption without examination that career planning means plotting a path for a top job. We say that your plan should not necessarily be a plot for a route to the top but a route to the kind of job and environment in which you will be happy. This usually means many things, such as:

1. Being useful.
2. Working in a field you like.
3. Having the respect of your peers.
4. Making enough money so that you have all of the necessities and many of the luxuries.
5. Having a good home situation.

Of that list, which can be quite long (if you really think about it), the most important is probably to work in a field you like. Many of you will say, "But I don't know what I will like because I've had limited work experience and I really don't know what jobs are like." Even so, you all should know what your personal likes and dislikes are, and a general rule is that you are most likely to be successful (by your own definition of success), if your own personal characteristics match up to a fair extent with the requirements of the job.

To get more specific, take as an example the jobs available in a manufacturing business for a person with engineering training. There are several functional areas, each with diverse job descriptions and opportunities where such a person might work if he is so inclined. What are these jobs?

In *manufacturing*, which is utilizing more and more college graduates, there is work in three major areas: (1) quality control, which usually now involves the design of sophisticated test equipment; (2) manufacturing engineering for manufacturing process expertise—welding, heat treating, plating, numerical control equipment; specification and purchase; production operations; and (3) line jobs such as foremen, superintendent, and plant manager.

In *marketing*—product planning, market research, application engineering at either the home office or in the field sales office.

In *finance*—data processing systems' operation and management.

Engineering itself has a great variety of kinds of work—research, advanced development design, factory liaison, production engineerng, engineering administration, and product service.

Kinds of work

What does the above have to do with personal characteristics? Well, here are a few examples of jobs and their major characteristics:

1. If a person is design-oriented and likes to work as a member of a team, then design engineering in the engineering function, or design of equipment in the quality control section of manufacturing are possibles.

2. If he likes a great deal of activity with a lot of short-time deadlines to meet, a high requirement for solving problems often and fast, and a great deal of interaction with people, then line manufacturing is a natural.

3. If you would rather work alone, be measured on your own output and have challenging creative problems, then research or development engineering may be your best bet.

4. If you want to really see what motivates our industrial system, with a job usually requiring a great deal of creativity in meeting customers' requirements or solving their problems within the constraints of your own company's capabilities, then marketing is a good place to be. But you must like people and, if they are customers, accommodate to *their* needs. Customers think it's their money they are spending and so they usually want things their way.

5. If you have a great deal of interest in computer applications and like the logic and approaches which go with them, then get into manufacturing production or scheduling; or the application of minicomputers to productivity improvements on the factory floor, or managing the computer center, or being a specialist in automated design.

6. A new kind of work called "product service" involves characteristics somewhat akin to manufacturing and engineering combined with customer contacts. Every industry has jobs in this category, though perhaps they are called by other names. But it involves troubleshooting usually on the customers' premises, has a very demanding time frame within which to operate—and for those who like these characteristics, a great deal of job satisfaction.

What does the above say? Simply that engineering-trained men and women can find satisfying work in some function of a business, that each kind of work has certain characteristics, and the choice is up to the person concerned. The idea is to fit the individual's skill and preference with the requirements of a job or position. The same principle holds for people trained in any discipline.

Kind of industry. Industries, too, have certain characteristics which can be identified by a little study. A career plan should include consideration of what kind of industry you believe you would be happy in and why. Using electrical engineering as an example, a person might consider going into power or electronics.

The power business, either public or private utility, is usually considered to be a mature industry. Its growth rate has been predictable. Recent events have thrown some disturbing factors into the situation, but it is still, and will be, a steadily growing industry. What else can be said about it? Well, utilities don't go bankrupt. They perform a most essential service and so are a controlled monopoly. As a monopoly they have the sole right to supply power to a geographical area and as a result are under government agency regulation, which of course poses some problems. But their business does not fluctuate widely and they do not have significantly large layoffs.

To say an industry is mature is not to say that it is devoid of new technological developments, for there are many, such as nuclear power, gas turbines, cryogenic transmission, and very high-voltage development.

On the other hand, the electronics industry, especially in the military and consumer areas, is very fast-moving and literally dynamic because of major technological developments. Brilliant young people who have a yen for a fast track would find this field attractive because of the rapid pace of these technological developments. But this industry still goes up and down with the economy, with wider swings than the power side, and, therefore, more chance for layoffs or disruptions. In between these two major categories are many other industries with characteristics somewhere in between.

The objective

There are a lot of old sayings about aiming high, on the basis that, if you do, you are more likely to achieve something that is satisfying than if your sights are set too low.

Career planning demands that, first, you set an objective, as modest or high as you wish—such as a professor or college president, a middle-management executive or the chief executive of a big company, or owner of your own company. You may decide to have multiple or alternative objectives. Next, plot the steps necessary to achieve that objective and the approximate time frame required. Again, to use the manufacturing industry example, it usually takes five to eight years of above-average work before a person is promoted to his first managerial job. In retailing, generally, or in a service industry, the first promotion may be as soon as 6 months or within the first 18 months after joining the company.

Note that a person should do *above-average* work. It should be both self-evident and logical that promotions will go to those who do above-average work rather than to those who do average or below-average. So the personal career plan which expects promotions should recognize this fact and act accordingly.

After the first promotion, the time frame is not quite as definite for the second or third, but it is usually shorter. In engineering it may be two to three years; in retailing, one to two years. When a person is tagged as a "comer" or PYM (promising young man), he is usually moved upward at shorter and shorter time intervals, provided he demonstrates capacity for intelligent, hard work. It is, however, quite true that in this world of ours today advancement down a chosen path is hard to come by on just a 40-hour week.

Small or large company?

It is good as part of a career plan to think through what the advantages and disadvantages might be to you of working for a large or a small company. The large one may give you more opportunities for work in different functional areas, perhaps more geographical areas, and usually access to formal training programs. The small company may give a good feeling of being closer to where the action is, more responsibility early in your career, and require you to be more of a generalist than a specialist. If formal in-house training programs do not exist in the small company, and they are felt to be necessary, they can always be obtained through nearby universities or through your technical or professional society. So, to repeat, there are pluses and minuses for small and large companies, but these are of importance only when measured against your own objectives and preferences and personal skills.

Geographical location

If you want to work overseas, there are certain companies which make such opportunities much more probable than other companies. The multinational corporation comes to mind at once, for the very designation identifies the scope of activity. Here, again, however, if you seriously want to work in some other countries, your plan should include some time scheduled to learn the foreign language of your choice, whether it be French, Spanish, Portuguese, German, or whatever.

The family

Few managers can be happy if their immediate family is not happy. So planning should take into account various family considerations of importance. If there are children, are the schools of the area considered adequate? Are religious facilities important and, if so, are they present? Is there any necessity to be near older parents or relatives so that their welfare can be monitored? It is true that many of these considerations are perhaps more important when one is middle-aged rather than just out of college, but they should be considered.

The long term

It is hard to disassociate oneself completely from the media— the newspapers, television, and particularly commentators. A recent speaker characterized it as, "Our daily dose of desperation dumped on us by the mass media in an enormous overkill to tell the tragedies of our time so that this beloved land has become the wailing wall of the world."

Certainly when we are in a recession it is not the end of the world, or even of our major industries, and if we have 8 percent unemployment it still means that 92 percent of our people are working. As recession abates, the economy gets healthier sooner or later. So do not be influenced by the near-term. Plan ahead for the next five to ten years as a minimum. No one knows precisely what the rates of growth will be, or when some of the growth industries will start their anticipated fast rises, but general agreement can be obtained on what the growth industries are, and what the mature industries are, and you *can* identify them, and you *can* lay your plans accordingly.

So don't take too seriously the prophets of gloom or the

prophets of boom, but do your own thinking—get competent advice—and plan. Neither recessions nor booms are permanent.

Sources of information

There are many sources of information, often unrecognized, regarding the nature and characteristics of work. They break down into the spoken word and the written word; that is, whether the information is obtained from talking to someone, or from publications. The question often uppermost in a person's mind is, "Just what does a person do in that job?" It could be the job of design engineer, buyer, public health nurse, loan officer, or whatever. The best source of information is from people who are now working or have worked in those jobs. They may be friends or acquaintances. A great deal can be learned by asking questions, and most people are very willing to talk about job requirements, characteristics, or specifications. The professional counselor at the high school, college, or employment agency is an official source of such information. One caution should be stated here, and that is that a great deal of data should be obtained before conclusions are drawn. Any one person may have a biased view of a job situation based on his own good or bad experiences. The conclusions of several people, however, should have a great deal of validity.

With regard to industry there are many good sources of information. The annual *Fortune 500* lists the major U.S. and foreign companies and their financial characteristics, together with some significant measurements. *Forbes* magazine in an annual issue gives five-year financial performances by company and by industry. In addition to just financial statistics, the U.S. business press (which has over 2,300 different publications) covers virtually every aspect of business and professional life. Over 160 individual areas are served, ranging from the mining and manufacturing industries to the service industries and the professions. In addition, the government has a very extensive list of publications covering many of the same areas. Librarians in both city libraries or in university libraries can guide a searcher to any published material.

Most large brokerage houses have research departments and

often specialize or follow a few industries. They issue reports summarizing prospects by industry category and, although they are aimed primarily at the investing community, are usually excellent overall treatments not only of the industry but also of the companies within the category. The reports can be very valuable for career planning because they not only give past and present financial data such as profits and growth rates, but also analyze future trends and projected growth rates. This latter data is not usually found in a municipal library or a liberal arts college library but in a business school library.

On changing jobs

The first job that a young graduate takes usually involves more hope than knowledge of the fit between the company and himself. So it is only natural that he often gets quite unhappy, or even disillusioned, with his situation after a short time. Many questions can then be asked, such as, "How long should a young person stay with his first job before he seriously considers finding a different job? How sure can he be that he is in the wrong job—are there any measurements to guide him? And, if by these criteria he is satisfied he should move, then how should he go about it? Should he tell his company he is dissatisfied and wants to move, or should he quietly look for another position? Should he write directly to other companies, or seek out the help of management placement men—'head hunters'?"

Generally speaking, a person should stay in his job, no matter how dissatisfied he is, for two years. After all, he chose or accepted the job. It does not speak well of his judgment or maturity if he gets disillusioned and moves in less than two years.

Before leaving a job where he is dissatisfied, a young manager should pinpoint the reasons for the move. In considering a new position, he should determine in what ways another job will be different—and better. Blindly jumping from one job to another seldom works out.

The authors' advice: Discover why the old job was unsatisfactory and determine why the new one will be better and satisfactory.

Quotations from three career plans

The authors believe nothing is so explanatory or real as the exact words written or spoken by individuals who are facing a challenge or problem. Following are quotations from three people who made out personal career plans before they started their business lives.

Career planner number one: Future career. This paper describes my personal aims and objectives as related to business and to my job career. My strengths and weaknesses, as I see them, are considered in achieving my goals and in performing my job. Then, I discuss various factors bearing on my future and the kind of product mix or balance among various interests which I desire. Finally, I comment on my feelings about such items as my responsibility and ethical position.

Aims and objectives. My career goals are (1) to work in a research position in the corporate development division of a large company, making studies of various industries and companies for acquisition purposes, and (2) within six years to be the head or manager of one of these acquired companies, or to return home to manage my family's business. My career plan is to learn the operations of a large company which is expanding quickly, and then to apply this knowledge and experience to a small business or company.

My personal objectives are (1) to continue my education with an MA in Economics and a CPA certificate, (2) to be well paid in my job and (3) to remain flexible so as to travel extensively in my job and during my vacations.

Therefore, I am looking for a job in corporate planning which will allow me to grow and progress to a management position, to continue my education, and to be well paid, with travel benefits. Education and travel are very important to me; I will be judging companies closely on these two aspects.

Strengths and weaknesses. In achieving the above goals, I recognize the following strengths and weaknesses in myself. First, strengths:

1. My greatest strength, I believe, is that I am a hard worker. I enjoy working and am bored if there is not enough work to

do. For this reason, I believe that a company will get its full value from me.

2. I am well organized and can get a great amount of work done in a short amount of time. I am reliable, and always meet deadlines.

3. I am independent and like to work by myself. This is why I think I am best fitted for a research position leading to a supervisory spot. When an assignment is made, I can and want to do it by myself. I do not need someone to watch over and prod me.

4. I am perceptive about people and size them up rather well, at least to my satisfaction. Therefore, I am not easily persuaded to join the "wrong" group, nor am I easily duped. This characteristic should be helpful in working with people when I move out of a staff position.

5. I have always been a strong-willed and positive type of person. Things have usually gone my way, and I have seldom failed at anything I have tried to do. I have a certain amount of self-confidence in knowing what I want to do and in knowing that I can do it.

6. I am flexible to move around, change jobs and locations to find the opportunity I want.

Counterbalancing my strengths, I have the following weaknesses:

1. I am a stubborn person. Sometimes my stubbornness limits my objectivity in reasoning, causing me to misjudge a situation.

2. I have only average intelligence, which means that in order to do better than average, I have to work harder.

3. I am too opinionated. Sometimes I state an opinion based on little exposure to the situation. I fail to give the other person a chance to present his side.

4. I find that my streak of independence often limits me in working with others or with a group; thus, I am not willing to accept another person's work without having a desire to check it. I will need to become more tolerant in my work.

5. I have some difficulty expressing myself orally, particularly

in front of a large group. Thus, I prefer a job in which the work will involve only a small group of people.

In general, I sum up my strengths and weaknesses by stating that I do have a strong personality and consider myself a strong person. I believe that my strengths and weaknesses stem from this central factor.

Factors to consider for the future. First, type of job. I have chosen a staff position in corporate planning for my initial job. I want a job in which I can make use of my economics and finance background. Also, I want the work to be varied and interesting and, as much as possible, independent.

Corporate planning has several features which interest me. First, it is a relatively new field and at this time, a great demand exists for people in this area. Second, the work varies from making economic studies of certain industries to deciding on the role of the board of directors in an acquired company to making financial studies on which companies to acquire. The job is not routine. Third, it is an excellent area in which to familiarize oneself with the workings of a company. This department usually works with an executive committee or the financial committee, so I would be in touch with top executives. Fourth, it is a good place in which to spot openings or positions in the operating management of an acquired company. This would be the final step in my career—managing a subsidiary. This step would be in lieu of managing my family's business.

I believe that heading in this direction will make the best use of my strengths and will allow me time to overcome my weaknesses and limitations. Although I will be working independently in a research position, I will nevertheless have some interplay with others and some work assigned to be done with others. This will require tolerance and patience on my part. Also, my reluctance to speak before groups will be alleviated by making presentations orally to my boss and to various committees. Thus, I consider the job outlined above ideal for preparing myself for a management position.

As for the type of company I am looking for:

1. Size—I want to work for a large corporation—one of the giants with sales of over $500 million. My choice of a large

company is because large companies have corporate planning departments, the type of work I want. Also, I think that a large company will offer more opportunity and a large company will be more formal and objective in its evaluation of my work.

2. Type of employer—The type of employer I desire is one who will be fair and helpful to me. I want to do my own work and to have as independent a job as is possible in a large organization. I want a boss to give me my instructions and assignment, my deadline, and then leave me alone to do the job. In this situation, I feel that I will do my best work and will enjoy it the most. I do not want the feeling of being watched and continuously having to explain what and why I am doing something. When I have completed my assignment, I then expect my employer to discuss its success or failure with me. I would welcome at that time all suggestions on how to improve my work.

3. Location—I have lived in New York City for a summer and liked it very much. Since most of the job opportunities for the type of position I want are in New York, this is my preferred location. However, I do not feel strongly about where I live and would be perfectly willing to move about and relocate. I want to travel in my job, if it is possible.

4. Hours of work—As pointed out in my strengths section, I consider myself a hard worker. In fact, unless I am working, I am bored. Therefore, I believe in working as long as is necessary to get the job done. I intend to work long hours, and will probably be attracted to a company which does some overtime work. I do not want a company which does not have enough work to do.

5. Compensation—Since I intend to do a sizable amount of work, I also intend to be paid well. I am just as interested in my initial salary as I am in my salary five or ten years from now. I want my salary to be competitive with others. The reasons I am interested in my initial salary are (1) I intend to avoid a regimented training program by demanding a higher salary, (2) I do not intend to work in a staff position for longer than ten years, so I want to skim the cream with this higher-paying position, and (3) I want to start off from a higher base for future raises. As far as promotions are concerned, I am more interested in salary promotions than in title promotions. I believe that if I can

reach the management level of an acquired company, I will be satisfied.

My product mix or balance of interests. Since I have never worked in business, I do not know what a real job is like. However, I would like to compare the school work and the job I do here to that of the business world. I do not think my interests and product mix will change radically when I begin my career from what they are now. Therefore, I can say that I will probably devote all of my time to my job—that I will definitely be overbalanced in favor of my work. At the present I have little to no social life or civic life, and few interests outside of my school work. And, I am happy with this situation.

Of course, if I were in a position which demanded or required community activities, I would participate. However, I would look on this as a part of my job, rather than a personal responsibility or interest. If I had to make a choice between my work and my other interests, I would choose my work.

My responsibilities will be to:

1. My employer—I choose my friends and associates carefully. There are not too many of them; however, the ones there are I am extremely loyal to. This is the same way I will approach my employer. As long as I feel that I have an opportunity to advance and grow in my job, I will be loyal. However, if I feel that I am being passed over, I will look for another job. As far as my responsibility to my work is concerned, I believe it is unnecessary to stress further that it will be unequalled.

2. Myself—To me, being responsible means utilizing my education and experience to the fullest extent. This is what I intend to do. If I did not do this, I would be cheating myself and my employer.

3. The community—At the present time I feel little responsibility toward the community. This could change over time, but right now such activities as the PTA, Community Chest, and so forth, hold no interest for me. I am not against them; I am neutral to them. As stated above, I would work with them if it were a part of my job. But as an individual interest, I would avoid them.

Ethical position. My ethical code is built around two factors— truthfulness and fairness. Although I consider myself to be ambitious, I am not so ambitious as to be unfair to someone else. There could be some conflict here, of course, but I think I would hold strongly to my ideas of fairness. Being of a conservative nature, I think my rules of fairness are about in line with the average person's. I do want to be respected, and I believe the best way to gain respect is to be fair.

I believe that if I make my future decisions with these two factors in mind, I will have little difficulty in justifying my ethical position. I might add that the only person whom I really care about satisfying ethically is myself, since I consider ethics to be a personal, individual matter.

Conclusions. In concluding this report, I want to wrap up my aims and objectives and what I want out of life with my personal image. A personal image is what others think of you; I hope that what I believe is my personal image and what others think of it will have some resemblance. I do not think I am either the tough guy or the nice guy, but in between, with a tendency toward the tough side. As stated above, I do not really care if people like me or not, but I do want to be respected and trusted. I want people to realize that when I say I will do something, that it will be done; that when I am told something in confidence, that it will remain in confidence. I believe that if I can gain the respect and trust of the people I work with, I will make a good employee, which will enable me to achieve my objectives.

Career planner number two. Before I plunge into the heart of this career plan paper, I feel that a brief introduction as to the sequence and contents of the areas covered will give you a better understanding of my ideas, beliefs, goals, strengths, and weaknesses, as presented. Basically, this paper will present my ultimate objective of life as well as two secondary objectives. Within the framework of each of these two secondary objectives will be my ambition concerning each objective. Having presented my objectives or goals and ambitions, I proceed to make a self-examination of my character in an effort to determine my basic strengths and weaknesses. In this area there are obviously innumerable aspects which could be cited; however, I have limited this paper to only those of the most significant nature. Upon analysis of myself, I found that there are certain areas in which there appears to be conflict and confusion on my part. Therefore, the third part of my paper deals with this conflicting area. Having examined my strengths, weaknesses, and conflicts in a somewhat isolated state, I proceed to relate these aspects to my objectives in determining whether my objectives are realistic. The final part of my paper concerns itself with the business future I have chosen and the sacrifice I will make, as well as the additional benefits to be derived from taking advantage of such an ideal opportunity.

There are many different philosophies professed by many different philosophers as to what should be the ultimate objective of life. The one philosophy which has had the most significant impact on my mind is that of Aristotle. According to the Aristotelian approach, the ultimate objective of life should be happiness. Although many people have a tendency to grasp this philosophy, perhaps because of its simplicity, most of them fail to clarify their meaning of the word "happiness." Therefore, in essence they fail to clearly define their objective of life. Recognizing the fact that Aristotle's definition of happiness, that being moral perfection and intellectual perfection would certainly be admirable goals, I feel that the present-day social, economic, and political situation makes this objective unrealistic. Therefore, in attempting to be more practical in my approach, I have adopted as my ultimate objective of life to making my family a healthy, happy, compatible, Christian unit. My parents have committed themselves to and practiced the same family objective. In other words, they truly live not for themselves but solely for my brothers and sisters and me. Having lived under this atmosphere, it naturally has had a positive influence on my feeling that my primary purpose for existence is to provide for my wife and children.

My background in relation to my economic security certainly has had a tremendous effect upon my philosophical outlook. Being a part of an affluent family has allowed me to recognize the lack of permanence of material possessions and has caused me to set my goals on a more permanent foundation such as the happiness of the family. However, had I not been exposed to these material possessions during my youth and recognized their lack of true meaning, I might have set my ultimate objective in terms of dollars rather than in the nonmaterialistic term of happiness.

Having established my ultimate objective, let us now turn to the nature of my secondary objectives and my ambitions within each objective. The first of these objectives I label as my "work objective." By nature of the fact that it is a secondary objective indicates that it is a means to an end rather than an end in itself. The basic thought here is that I would not be willing to sacrifice any obligations at home in order to increase my availability for work unless it would be to the betterment of my family in the long run. For example, in considering the situation, I would not have accepted the additional territory if I felt that my absence would have created undue frustration and emotional disharmony within the family unit. However, if I had felt that by accepting this additional responsibility my family would have been much better off in the long run—that is, successful raise in salary thus allowing me to give my family more economic security—then I would have accepted it.

In relation to my working environment, there are several desires which if fulfilled would make an ideal situation. The work must be continually challenging and it must offer me an opportunity to see my accomplishments as worthwhile. In other words, my work must not be of an insignificant, routine nature where its completion is really of no great significance. Following the same line of reasoning, my work should give me economic power and social prestige. The major reason for wanting to attain strong economic power is two-fold. First, although the degree of economic security one desires varies among individuals, for my own purpose, I feel that I must have a substantial amount. I would like to be economically secure enough so that the availability of money would not be the determining factor in attempting to satisfy my family's desires for any material possessions within reason (i.e., $300,000 home—reasonable—as opposed to a $1,000,000 home—unreasonable). Second, I want economic independence in order that I can stand up for what I think is right without having to "tailor" my views because my economic supporters feel otherwise. This second reason for wanting economic security is magnified when analyzed in light of my political objective of becoming a U.S. Senator after I become mature. The final desire I have concerning my future environment is that I live in _____. I have lived there for many years and have grown to love its people. You can understand my close attachment to the community by the fact that we are one of the city's oldest and most prominent families. More important than the social prominence is that I feel that _____ will provide an excellent atmosphere for raising my family. Obviously, this latter point is directly in line with my ultimate objective of life-family happiness. As far as my ambition in business is concerned, it is to become co-owner (with my brother) of my father's business and to manage it as successfully as my father has done to date.

Having determined my ultimate objective of life and my secondary objective, I will proceed to enumerate the areas in which I feel I am particularly strong. I consider myself to have a pleasing personality with an exceptional ability to meet and talk with people, regardless of their social status or professional background. Not only am I especially adept in making friends, but I also have an ability to communicate my ideas well. In relation to working with other people, I have never had any significant difficulty in this area. One major strength which I do have in the interpersonal area is that I am able to organize and delegate the work that must be done. This ability to delegate is to my mind of essence in being successful in the business world. I operate under the old philosophy that each man can just do a limited amount of work, therefore the only way to be economically successful is "to earn money off the sweat of the other man's brow." It is under this philosophy that delegation of work becomes essential.

A second major strength which I feel I possess is that of ambition. I have a strong desire to accept responsibility and to see that a job is carried out properly. If I have a job to do, I don't procrastinate, but rather I get it done, irrespective of its difficulty. Although I have this desire for responsibility, the overriding factor in determining whether or not to accept additional responsibility is the possible detrimental effects on the happiness of my family. For example, if I were a district sales-manager and were given an opportunity to advance to a more responsible position of regional manager, but because of this advancement my family would be unable to make the necessary environment adjustment (i.e., move), then I would not accept the new position.

A third major strength which I possess is that of organizing and planning my work. In other words, I plan ahead and do not commit myself on the spur of the moment. I don't do what is best in the short run or at a particular moment in time without giving full consideration for the ramifications of the decision on my future. This, I feel, is an advantageous characteristic because it not only enables you to make more rational decisions, but it will enable you to gain more confidence from your subordinates by their knowing that their superior is a well-organized individual.

The final major area of strength which I possess is that of education. I feel that I have received a fine education. However, the strength of this education doesn't rest upon the reputation of the institutions, but upon my using these institutions in developing a "problem-solving, analytical mind." From the academic training of each of the schools I have attended, I feel that I have developed a skill for recognizing the major problems in a complex situation, selecting alternative courses of action, and making logical decisions with specific plans, actions, and recommendations as solutions. Therefore, the education itself is not an end in itself but rather the means to an end, that being developing a problem-solving, analytical mind to apply to any situation—be it social, business, or political.

In relation to my weaknesses, I feel that my major one is that I use people as a means to an end; that end being, the betterment of myself. This is certainly a basic weakness in that once a person has acquired this reputation other people become extremely skeptical about working with him. Also, I feel that it is unethical to use people as a means to whatever end you desire without their recognizing your full intentions. If, however, they do clearly understand your intentions concerning themselves, then I feel that my using them is justified.

A second major weakness which I possess is the fear of failure. I always want to do the right thing at the right time and constantly have a fear of failing to do it. For example, in a classroom discussion I will not present my points which have a bearing on the discussion for fear of being wrong. At the same time, I recognize that one of the best ways to learn is from your mistakes, but I still can't muster up enough courage to present my points. As I examine myself, I guess the basis for such idiotic action stems from my extreme egotism and pride. In striving to never make mistakes, I fail to commit myself on anything of which I am not certain. Along the same line, a third major weakness which I possess is that I have an extremely strong desire for prestige and status. These desires are not in themselves weaknesses, but they become so when they begin to undermine one's behavior. In other words, my desire for prestige and status tends to become the major factor in my decision making. Perhaps this weakness exists because of my lack of maturity. I certainly hope that it will not remain with me forever, for this egotism is diametrically opposed to my ultimate objective of life, where I place my family, not myself, as the sole unit to live and provide for.

A fourth weakness which is of significant importance in the business environment is my inability to project a commanding image and thereby gain authority. If I were going to work for someone other than my father, this weakness would become magnified. However, because of my position within his company, coupled with my economic power, my image will gain significant materialistic support, which in itself can project a great deal of authority.

A fifth weakness which I possess is my failure to realize that people in the business world will really "screw you" if they get the chance. As a result of my somewhat naive approach, I will initially be pushed around. However, because I will be working under my father, who is extremely cut-throat when necessary, hopefully I will quickly become cognizant of "how the real world functions as opposed to the assumptions made at universities."

Examining my strengths and weaknesses in light of my stated objectives, I don't feel that my goals and aspirations are unreasonable or unattainable. At the present, I feel that my best chance for accomplishing my outlined objectives is by working for my father, who owns and operates several stores throughout the Northwest. The company is extremely progressive. Also, I feel that I would enjoy working with the company executives because they are well educated and socially attuned. Although I am not particularly in love with the store business, the opportunity available appears to me to be ideal. The president of the company had decided (primarily because he is my father), to take me under his wing as his protégé and teach me the business, while compensating me both by salary and by ownership in the company, both of which will amount to a rather handsome compensation. My income will provide an excellent security factor, which is the paramount means by which I will accomplish my objectives. These earnings will allow me to accumulate the economic power and economic prestige that will be necessary in accomplishing my political objective of becoming a U.S. Senator, as well as give me definite economic security for my family. I could perhaps work for other people doing other functions which presumably would be more enjoyable from a working environment point of view, but, at the same time, it would be virtually impossible for me to attain the equivalent compensation while working in these more enjoyable positions. Therefore, in light of my objectives, I am willing to sacrifice the everyday working satisfaction for having this additional economic security.

An advisor who read this career plan said, in part, to its writer:

1. It is good to read of your political ambitions.
2. Why do you assume the business world is so cut-throat and the nice guy always gets taken? Wouldn't you think that business is much like people, some nice and decent while others . . . ?
3. Don't worry about mistakes, Babe Ruth hit 60 in 1927 but struck out over 100 times that year. They won't pay you a dime if you don't get the bat off your shoulder and take your cuts. From there on it's just a matter of averages.
4. So much of this lack of confidence and fear of making an ass of oneself is purely sensitivity and, as you say, egotistical pride. All of us suffer from it but few of us do anything about it. Good luck.

Career planner number three. I approach my career planning just as I would examine and analyze a business and its management. First of all, I will examine my assets. Against these assets I will weigh my liabilities and arrive at a net worth.

Since the above net worth is in part attributable to my past actions, and these actions are the result of my goals, ambitions, and so forth, I will then examine these goals and ambitions along with my beliefs and attitudes. One result should be a good insight into where I have been, and why I am where I am now. The most important result, however, will be my projection of where I could get and where I want to get in the future.

Assets. I consider one of my most important assets to be the fact that I know what I want in life.

My wife ranks equally with the above as an important asset. She not only shares my desires to achieve my previously formulated goals but has been and will be a great help in achieving these goals. She and I are able to freely discuss all subjects. She has unselfishly taught school for the past two years to obtain the financial resources so that I could continue my education. She will be an excellent hostess for business and social affairs.

My other assets are more common and have to do with my general abilities and personality.

I am an intelligent individual. According to my IQ, I have above-average intelligence. This is a distinct asset as it places me above the crowd and gives me a head start in achieving my goals.

I know how to apply this intelligence. I enjoy hard and challenging work. I don't mind tackling a tough assignment because I know I can handle it. I don't make a show of this intelligence when working with others of lesser intelligence.

I have a "sense of responsibility." This "sense" is hard to define and is best described by example. It is the feeling that I have when hired or asked to do a job. I feel that other people are depending on me to do the best job that I can and thus I am not satisfied until I have completed the job to the best of my ability.

While in the Navy I felt it was my obligation and responsibility to do my best. And not for just 8 hours a day but 24 hours a day if necessary. Many junior officers rationalized that since they were making only a small amount per month they would give the Navy only that much worth of work. Thus they performed second-rate work.

My biggest challenge was as chief engineer of an LST. The ship had unique engineering problems in addition to a poorly disciplined crew. I came aboard and decided that I would set as my goal the winning of the "Red E" for engineering excellence. It took 14 months of 24-hour-a-day work, but I whipped the crew into shape and won it.

There was no reward for doing a good job. There is no bonus for a job well done and I knew that it would have no effect on my promotion schedule—I was getting out of the Navy a year before I could possibly be advanced to the next rank. My motivation was simply this "sense of responsibility," and the desire to do a good job.

I do not mind hard work. In fact, I enjoy hard work and plenty of it. I would rather be overworked than underworked. When underworked and with time on my hands, I get restless and bored and tend to lose interest in what I am doing.

As shown by the Navy example above, I take pride in my work and try to do a job to the best of my ability.

The above four factors—my intelligence, my sense of responsibility, my fondness for hard work, and my pride in my work—can be lumped together in a single package which I shall call my "work potential." If an employer is looking for a man possessing this potential, I feel that my work potential is above average and thus will be a distinct asset to me.

As far as my personality is concerned, I feel that it is an asset, too. To be specific, I am easy to get along with and have no trouble getting along with others, whether they are the upper crust of highest New York society or the indigent coal miners and/or farmers from the backwoods. I enjoy meeting and talking with people but choose my close friends with care. I am quiet and reserved but not aloof. I do not believe in backslapping and skylarking but enjoy conversation with all types of people.

Finally, I believe in standing up for my beliefs. If I believe I am right, I will argue in spite of overwhelming opposition. I do not switch sides depending on which way the tide is running. And I have little respect for wishy-washy people who do.

In arriving at the above beliefs or positions, I do not come to hasty decisions. I take a stand only after carefully weighing the pros and cons of the issue and after much deliberation. This should not be construed as meaning that I am a man of indecision—one who continually weighs the pros and cons of an issue and can never reach a decision. On the contrary, once I feel that I have examined the issue fully I reach my decision and stand ready to defend it.

My selection of a job for next year is an excellent example of this positive decision-making process. I carefully and deliberately weighed the pros and cons of five different offers, taking into account my goals, ambitions, desires, and abilities, and made a decision. I then wrote one letter of acceptance and four refusals and am ready to go to work on 15 September. (As a matter of interest, I am already studying company and trade literature to get a head start on my job.)

I could have delayed my decision for another month or so, but would have accomplished nothing by doing so. I knew what I wanted and where I could get it, so there was no reason to delay.

Liabilities. I have three main liabilities which tend to negate the above assets to a degree.

My most serious is the fact that I am not a "deep thinker." I am a "nuts and bolts" man rather than a philosopher. This is partially a result of my engineering training, where ideas can be stated in the form of definite equations and the solutions to the equations are definite quantities. I realized this deficiency while I was still in engineering school and my decision to do graduate business work was based partially on the desire to correct it. I feel that I have made substantial progress in becoming a deeper thinker in the past year and a half but still have a long way to go.

My second liability is the fact that I am not articulate and have a difficult time expressing myself. Although my point may be clearly defined and well thought out in my mind, because of my lack of expressiveness I often fail to get it across. My goal is to develop a command of the English language and the ability to express myself well.

This difficulty in expressing myself has affected my participation in certain discussions. Though I am not satisfied, I have improved noticeably in my ability to express myself.

The case method, which is based on free group discussion, has been invaluable to me. I had never been in a situation where I was called upon to express my ideas. All classes in engineering school were lecture or lab, with no class discussion.

This difficulty of self-expression is not confined to oral presentations. I also have a difficult time with papers. However, I have made an improvement lately but there is still much work to be done.

My third main liability is my tendency to rely too heavily at times on my intelligence to pull me through a given situation. Thus I enter the situation slightly less than fully prepared. I expect to play it by ear as the situation progresses.

I do this because I don't want to waste time doing unnecessary work. Rather than spend my time on this work, I have other equally important things to do—namely, obligations to wife and family, outside activities such as Navy Reserve, and so forth. In other words, I try to spread myself too thin. Occasionally, it catches up with me.

Before netting out assets and liabilities to determine my net worth, there is one additional characteristic which could be classified as either an asset or a liability. This is my easygoing nature. This characteristic is difficult to classify because it works to my advantage at times and at times to my disadvantage. Because thus far it has worked to my advantage, I will call it an asset, but note that it is a potential liability.

I attribute much of my success in life to this easygoing attitude. But I might have been more successful had I had less of an easygoing nature. To illustrate—I attribute much of my success ("success" defined as learning much and making good grades, yet at the same time enjoying a happy and full social and family life) to my ability to minimize problems and not worry about future assignments and/or past poor performances. I am concerned about it but do not worry. For me, the MBA experience has been an enjoyable one—two years well and happily spent. For some people who let future assignments and/or past problems worry them, however, it has been a two-year nightmare and the effect of this nightmare is apparent on their attitude, performance, physical condition, and family life.

With my easygoing nature, I tend to procrastinate at times but have never been late in performing a job that was assigned to me.

Net worth. Very little summing up is needed because I have explained my liabilities in light of my assets, and vice versa.

The fact that I realize my most serious liabilities—my lack of ability to express myself and to think deeply—and am striving to correct them is important. I hope to turn this liability into an asset.

With my easygoing disposition, I feel I strike the proper balance between concern and happiness. However, I must continue to realize it can be a liability in some situations.

All in all, I feel that my assets far outweigh my liabilities and that the resulting net worth is extremely attractive and merchantable when viewed as the means for achieving my particular goals and ambitions in life.

Goals and ambitions. My goals and ambitions in life are simple and concisely stated:

1. To have a happy and successful family and home life.
2. To find a challenging and enjoyable business position that will utilize my abilities and will pay me enough to sustain this happy home life.

My idea of a happy home life is again fairly simple. I am a simple man with simple tastes. I do not enjoy the social rat race where life is a series of cocktail and dinner parties. My idea of an enjoyable evening out is:

1. Cocktails at home with a few close friends.
2. Dinner with same friends at quiet downtown restaurant or country club.
3. Back home without friends by 10:30 or 11:00.
4. Read good book until 11:30.
5. Asleep by 11:30 so that I can arise at 6:00-6:30 to enjoy the beauty of early morning.

My idea of an enjoyable week night is:

1. Home from work by 6:00-6:30.
2. Drink before dinner with wife from 6:30-7:00.
3. Dinner 7:00-8:00.
4. Read good book or work in shop at hobby or discuss problems of day with wife 8:00-10:00.
5. In bed and asleep by 10:30.

I plan to spend at least half a day on Saturday and all day Sunday with wife and family.

My house will be simple yet functional. Four bedrooms, three baths, den, several fireplaces but above all surrounded by at least ten acres of land on which I can keep a horse. I am an outdoors man and prefer the simple "small-town" life to the sophisticated life which I shall refer to as the "big-city" life.

I want to be regarded by my wife, family, and friends as a good husband, father, and friend. I feel that the above goals and actions will result in this.

My business goal is to find a position that will enable me to have this happy home life. Just any position is not satisfactory, however. It must be enjoyable, a challenge, and it must utilize my abilities. These abilities were summed up as my net worth and include both my business and engineering training.

Above all, I want to be regarded by my business associates as being:

1. A competent businessman.
2. A gentleman.
3. A good friend.

I want a position with responsibility and authority soon—not after 10 to 15 years, but within 1 or 2 years. I feel that I can handle such a position and want the opportunity to prove so.

Ultimately, I want to be the president of a small business, or have my own business. I will need a good salary.

I realize that at times my business goals and home life desires may conflict. I may have to sacrifice one to have the other, but I hope that it will be a temporary sacrifice. For instance, for three or four years when first starting my business career I will have to work hard and perhaps extra hours to achieve a desired position. Thus I will not be able to spend the time I would like with my family. But this is a short-range inconvenience which must be endured to achieve long-range happiness. And in later life, when I achieve my goal of president, I may have to entertain and attend cocktail parties for business reasons. But I hope to find a position which will require a minimum number of compromises of this type.

Beliefs. The majority of my beliefs should be evident from the preceding discussions.

First of all, I believe in living every minute of life as it comes. I enjoy the bad with the good, realizing that the unpleasant occurrences will soon be forgotten, leaving only fond memories of good times. Life is too short to spend your time wishing away the present while waiting for the future. To illustrate, I had a friend in the Navy who disliked it violently and spent his whole three years wishing for the end of his tour to arrive. As a result the three years were misery and will remain in his mind as three miserable years.

Next, I am a gentleman and believe that all transactions both personal and business must be strictly honest and on a high moral and ethical plane. I will not have it any other way. I believe in individual freedom. I believe that each man should make his own opportunities—not be handed them (in the form of a welfare check or a guaranteed annual wage). This destroys the free enterprise system on which this country was founded.

I believe that I have certain civic and individual responsibilities. I do not intend to be a national crusader for the conservative movement because I will not have the time and/or resources and because I am not the type of spokesman the movement needs. They need a more articulate individual. I do intend to promote conservatism on the grassroots level among my group of friends and associates by pointing out the dangers of liberalism and the advantages of conservatism. If there are enough of us on the grassroots level, we may someday swing the tide of political thinking.

I also intend to *work with,* not just belong to the Jaycees, Rotary Club, and so forth, in their projects for civic betterment.

I intend to remain in the Navy Reserve because I enjoy it and, more important, I feel that I can serve the country usefully through the Reserve.

Although I am an honest, moral, and ethical man, I am not a deeply religious man. I have trouble resolving the teachings of the Bible with my business beliefs concerning competition and tough selling. This is an unresolved conflict with which I have been struggling for some time and which will take a lot more thought.

Summary by the authors

A career does not have to be largely at the mercy of the economic winds that blow. We all know there is an element of chance or luck that holds, but it's not the 50 percent often mentioned. There is more than a suspicion that luck favors the person who does the planning. Pasteur said fortune favors the prepared mind.

The plan should include the family. It should be long-term. True enough, there is a short-term requirement to get a job and, if the economy is not booming, you may not be able to get the ideal job of your choice. But you can always make the move later if you know what it is you want.

Find the kind of work you like, because you will automatically be better at it. To do this you *must* decide what you like. Though we favor planning, we also raise a little caution regarding it. Steve Bechtel, head of the very large contracting and consulting company which bears his name, was asked: "What advice would you give to a son or daughter as he or she starts a career?" He replied: "Decide which industry appeals to you. Then pick the company you will want to be associated with, learn the business. If you are with a good outfit, the company will look after you. Too many young people go too far in trying to plot their own course."

We agree with Bechtel that it is possible to go overboard on planning, but do *some,* as discussed in this chapter. We believe your plan should be written out. It should include alternate paths, and should have flexibility. It should be updated regularly, at least annually.

If such a plan is developed, it gives the developer some basis for making decisions when they are called for. When a person is offered a transfer in his own company, or a job outside the company, great anxiety is often generated on whether to accept or not. Whereas if a plan has at least been generated once, the first question which one can ask himself is, "Is this new job in accord with, and taking me down the road of my own career plan?" If it is, fine; if not, the analysis can go forward with a clearer delineation of the pros and cons.

Finally here are some Hammaker observations that relate to "managing yourself."

1. To get ahead, understand yourself and itemize your strengths and weaknesses. Determine your ambitions—what you want to become in all phases of your life. Establish priorities within and outside of your business.

2. Understand as best you can all of those people who are of great importance to you including your bosses, your peers, your subordinates, your family, your friends. Determine how you can "assist" your boss to meet his ambitions and to be useful rather than harmful to your peers. Create a climate favorable to the self-development of your subordinates. Cooperatively, with your family, build a "good" life.

3. In business, understand the objectives, the processes, the procedures, the problems, the markets, the competitors, the outside influences and how you are to be judged. By analysis, through conversation, by reading, by listening to your bosses, subordinates, customers, and others, bring into focus and order on a priority basis problems and solutions, opportunities and ways to cash in on them.

4. Build a rationale for your solutions and ideas so that you are able to *persuade* your boss, associates, subordinates, customers, and others that your idea or solution is practical. Also be able to persuade them to adopt your solutions or ideas. They will be beneficial to them over the long run. If your proposals won't benefit all groups, make sure that they do benefit the business and the groups most important to you and, if possible, not "turn off" others.

5. Wherever and whenever it is feasible in your situation to do so, work on a consultative, participative basis with those reporting to you. Doing so will produce some good ideas, alert you to some dangers, and after the idea or solution is arrived at you will find some of the most important people are persuaded.

They in turn will help you to persuade others as to the merit of your proposals.

6. A touchstone for success in many, if not all, businesses is to think and act as a proprietor. Plan and spend capital and expense dollars, implement your plans, treat your people as you would in your own business. If you can't do this because of company policy or the general climate or other reasons, we recommend that you work to create a situation and climate where acting as proprietor is both acceptable and prized. Acting as a proprietor in most cases *persuades* your boss that you have a deep and genuine interest in the business. If the proprietor's idea isn't practical you can still behave in a thoroughly responsible manner.

7. Be sure to let the people reporting to you know what's going on before they read it in the company paper or the newspaper. Examples are giving them advance information on monthly sales, quarterly profits, new products, and acquisitions.

8. Have fun or at least really enjoy your work.

9. Never let your boss be surprised. Keep him informed on both good and bad developments. Managers who really know what is going on can do this. Don't accept surprises from your people.

10. Don't be self-centered. Have a genuine interest in your boss, superiors, peers, customers, family, and friends. Listen to them. Try to understand them. Play back what they say to you. Do listen intently and give the individual speaking to you your undivided attention. This is the greatest compliment possible.

11. I expect most really successful executives know how to manage their time. It is a neat trick to be available to your boss, your subordinates, and others to do the required routine and ceremonial things and still find time to think, to plan, to act, so that you make, as an individual, a personal, significant contribution to the success of your business.

12. Be a leader. Not all bosses are. Bosses are appointed. They have rank and power. Leaders, in addition, earn their leadership role. Leaders have followers who follow on a "voluntary" basis. Leaders have objectives. These objectives are "bought" by followers. The leader and his objectives create unity—a sense of purpose. They gain commitment. Aside from

self-motivation the leader/follower motivation is the best. Assuming good objectives and ability on the part of the leader, this produces a superior result.

If the 100 or 1,000 or 10,000 or 100,000 people employed by a given company work just 3 percent or 4 percent or 5 percent or 6 percent or 7 percent more effectively than a similar number employed by a competitor, the economic results of the first concern will be significantly better, and most likely the workers will be pleased or proud to be a part of a company that excels.

13. Don't cut corners.

14. Earn a profit for the company and for yourself.

15. Men/women of belief, conviction, integrity, with inquiring minds, common sense and continuing enthusiasm can become greater than most can imagine. The most important matter after survival is what *we can become.*

A manager can keep his integrity and succeed in business. (See question 37 and answer.)

It is almost impossible for a manager who lacks self-confidence to achieve much success. (See question 40 and answer.)

The more you know about your business and your industry, the greater your chance of being quite successful, if you also practice the six managing principles covered in Chapters 3, 5, 6, 7, 8, 9. (See question 53 and answer.)

Paul M. Hammaker

There are many unwritten laws of business, from how to treat the boss's secretary to training a successor, which are seldom discussed and are treated in the category of common sense. But most common sense is derived from experience and young managers have not yet accumulated either.

Louis T. Rader

appendix

*56 questions young managers ask
and answers by the authors*

Thirty years ago the American Society of Mechanical Engineers published in their journal several articles on "The Unwritten Laws of Engineering." This series received national recognition and has been and still is reprinted and distributed at major student meetings. Why was it so successful? Because it treated many areas which contribute to success but which the young engineer knew essentially nothing about. These included such matters as appropriate dress as well as behavior principles such as protecting the boss, not intruding into other peoples' responsibilities, and doing whatever necessary to get the job done.

Lacking among all the formal principles of management and behavior is a recognition that many problems of this type exist and are troublesome to young managers—sometimes because they have never even realized there was a problem and perhaps more often because they had no basis for knowing what good practice might be. They have had no relevant experience to guide them and their formal education probably did not cover the problems.

Some of these areas of importance to the young manager follow in a question and answer format. They include relations with his own manager, relations with his own employees, relations with other company employees, attitude toward company problems, optional behavior, and knowledge of business.

The young manager's relations with his own manager

1. Is his main job to understand his people or his manager?

A. If he doesn't understand his manager, he won't be around long enough to understand his people.

2. How important is it to treat his manager's secretary with respect and wariness/carefulness?

A. It is very important, and you better believe it. Most young managers do not appreciate how much their manager's secretary can either help or hurt them. They should treat her with kid gloves. If she is a long-term occupant of the spot, her influence is correspondingly greater.

3. Under what circumstances should he either get to see his manager immediately or be certain that his manager gets a message from him also immediately?

A. Whenever any incident occurs which could put his manager in a bad light with his boss. This could be an irate customer with a complaint where the customer may go, or has gone, to register his complaint top-side; or a failure to achieve a major and promised objective—whether a large order, or an unsuccessful bid; or a seriously injured employee. In no case should the young manager's manager be left ignorant of any adverse incident which his boss might call him about. Young managers who protect their boss are themselves protected.

4. How should the young manager tell his employee that the latter's request for some deviation of normal practice has been turned down? Should he say, "They have decided it would be a precedent"?

A. No, he should make the employee feel that he was a full party to the decisions. If he does not, the employee may believe the young manager does not really believe in his superior's decision or that he is merely a go-between with no real authority or knowledge of company procedures, both of which would be bad. It destroys his own authority, undermines the employee's respect for him, and suggests that the young manager instead of having responsibility and authority is only a figurehead.

5. If a young manager wants a raise for one of his personnel or wants to promote one of his people, should he tell him that he is going to recommend it before he does? If it is turned down should he say, "They won't let me give you more money or the better job"?

A. This is one of the most common errors made by a new, young manager—to tell his personnel in advance what his proposed action will be when it needs higher approval. He has everything to lose and nothing to gain. He must not curry favor with his employees by implying or promising raises or advancements and then, if they don't develop, blame upper management or someone else in the company such as a salary administration specialist.

6. A young manager said: In my new job I have worked very hard but have received virtually no guidance from my boss. What should I do?

A. If the boss won't help, there are often other experienced people in the office or shop or store who can and will help a new person if he asks for it. There is no stigma attached to asking for help; in fact, it is usually taken as a tribute by the person solicited.

7. A young manager asked: Should I aspire to my boss's job?

A. Of course, if you want it, but the rule is to push him upward not downward.

8. Should I make my boss look good? If he is promoted will it be good for me?

A. An emphatic *yes* and *yes.* If you make your boss look good, he'll make you look good, and vice versa.

9. How far does a young professional go in deciding which is more important to do first—his own jobs, or one his boss gives him? Should he always ask when he gets an assignment when the due date is? Should he generally, or always, give a boss's request top priority?

A. As a rule, accept the boss's priority. Basically he has the power to reward or punish. An engineering manager asked a young engineer to do a job which would have taken three or four hours. A few days later when he asked the young man if he had the job done, the latter said, "No I just haven't had enough time yet to get to it." Replied the engineering manager, "Don't tell me you haven't had enough time, for you have had plenty. Each of us always has the same amount—24 hours in a day. Instead, tell me that there were other things you wanted to do that you felt were more important than the job I gave you."

10. Can one mistake which the boss sees clearly, jeopardize a budding career? What is the possibility of being fired for a few mistakes?

A. These concerns may be addressed by considering the risk inherent in a managerial job as a function of the level of the job. The risk is proportional to the level. At the lower level, such as a foreman or product engineering manager, the risk is relatively low. The job is structured, there is not a great deal of discretion involved in lower-level jobs, there is usually little contact with people outside the company. The higher a management level is, the more risk there is in the job, simply because more resources are involved, mistakes will be more serious, and at the same time the higher-level managers are older and have more experience.

Our experience and conviction is that young managers tend to worry too much about mistakes they may make in the early days of their career. Higher-level management have themselves worked their way up, have themselves made mistakes which they clearly remember, and they know younger men lack experience. In fact, some say openly that young men are entitled to some mistakes—if they make none, they are probably not trying hard enough, are not aggressive, are not trying to plow new ground. Management does not penalize or fire young managers for a few errors. They actually look upon errors as indications of the necessary education by the younger men; they use them for coaching and teaching. Young men often forget that their bosses want them to succeed, to be useful and valuable to the company and themselves, and to grow.

It is true of course that management doesn't want the same mistake made by the same people too often. And the nature of the mistake has some bearing. If the young manager pretty clearly did not do his homework or did not show reasonable

diligence in unearthing the facts, he will probably have this
pointed out to him. If the error occurs because of poor judgment when he had the facts, this is a little more serious, but is
not a threat to the man's career unless it recurs often. The
man's attitude must also be good. He must recognize and
acknowledge the mistake and take pains not to make the same
mistake again. Under no circumstances, however, should the
young manager be less aggressive or hard working or ambitious
simply to avoid ever making a mistake.

11. To what extent should he encourage the people reporting
to him to be critical of the company, himself or fellow workers?

A. Usually this is a very dangerous thing to do. A supervisor
who encourages spying, tattling, bad-mouthing of the company or
of others, or derogatory comments will attract a certain class of
employee to him and will have real trouble separating fact from
fiction. On the other hand, he needs the truth if he is to operate
satisfactorily and this must be obtained from people. He must
make sure that people are criticizing the situation or the results,
and that such criticisms are constructive. He cannot afford to
encourage or entertain criticisms of one employee by another.
(This relates to the *Law of the Situation* by Mary Parker
Follett.)

12. To what extent should the young manager support and
defend the people reporting to him when they are under fire?
Does it make any difference whether they are "right" or
"wrong"?

A. When one of his employees is criticized for anything, the
young manager should neither believe nor reject the criticism
out of hand. He should promise to look into it and should do
so. If there is another side to the story, and there usually is, he
should get it and carry it back to the original criticizer. If his
employee is indeed in error, he should talk with him and again
acknowledge to his informant the accuracy of his information
and the action he has taken. This way he does not turn off
information which may help his component to perform more
efficiently nor does he lose the confidence of his people on the
basis that he will believe anything bad about them.

13. Should the young manager tell his people what went on
at the staff meeting?

A. Generally, the more employees know about the problems and plans of a business, the more they feel a part of it. They should be told anything—good or bad—provided that there is no restriction against passing on information and it does not hurt their attitude to the company. Often the more an employee knows about his manager's problems, the more he can help him by making better decisions himself. Information which would put any other manager or employee in a bad light or which would indicate vacillation or politics, or anything questionable or threatening should not be repeated. People like to be on the inside and the real way to make them feel on the inside is to give them data. They must also be told anything which affects them or their company before they read it in the paper.

14. If the young manager has an employee whom he knows to be bright and able and in a job he should be able to do well, but the employee's performance is poor, how long should he wait before he does anything and what should he do?

A. One of the most common mistakes in this situation is to wait too long. He shouldn't wait very long. As soon as he has more than one incident of unsatisfactory work, he should talk to the employee—not accusingly or threateningly, but openly and calmly to see if he can find out what the problem is—for there often is one. Then he should continue to talk to the employee whenever he sees evidence of bad or good work. Only after a fair amount of this kind of counseling and supervision should any thought be given to transferring him out. If the supervisor does nothing about poor work, or waits too long to do something, the efficiency of some others in his component will go down because they see someone getting away with low-level performance without penalty.

15. Should the young manager always be available to his people?

A. Most of the time, yes, but it is satisfactory to reserve some stated time for yourself alone. This should not be excessive, for often all progress stops while people wait to see the boss.

16. What are enough and not too many meetings?

A. Staff meetings are usually held weekly. During critical problems, meetings may be held daily, but in this case they must almost never be over an hour long. (Meetings are discussed in detail in Chapter 5.)

17. As a young manager, how do I establish a standard system of measuring performance when so many of my people are obviously better in one part of their job than another; for example, an employee in a bank is responsible for both selling services and making loans, but may be much better in one area than the other.

A. Since the job involves more than one type of work, you establish the relative importance for each type and, in effect, establish a point system. This decision concerning relative importance should be based on your judgment and should reflect the views of your boss also. If they conflict, you must resolve the conflict, based on discussions with your boss. It is then essential that all employees in this category understand the system and get regular feedback on their performance.

18. Can I change people reporting to me so they become better people?

A. Yes you can if you apply the principles and ideas covered in Chapters 3 through 12.

19. If I get a suggestion from my people, should I point out to them its good features only?

A. Heavens, no! Try to evaluate both good and bad, otherwise they will eventually have little respect for your judgment or reasoning ability—but it must be done carefully so that suggestions are not turned off.

20. My boss told me that I cluttered my talking with "pat" expressions that had become monotonous and even irritating to him and others. He told me to correct this fault. How do I get at this problem?

A. Too many people unknowingly form a habit where they use with monotonous predictability such phrases as, "You know . . . ," "I feel like . . . ," "You see . . . ," "Now let me tell you . . . ," "In all my years of experience, I never . . . ." A sure and frightening remedy for this habit is to get someone to tape a few of your conversations. Because these habits carry over to our home life, you can get your wife or husband to do one and play it back for you. If you are amazed, you can quickly prepare a self-administered remedy which will enable you to eliminate this problem.

21. My boss told me unless I became a better communicator my growth in responsibility and pay would be limited. Do managers really get penalized if they are or are rated as poor communicators?

A. Very much so and, indeed, the opposite is true also. In our executive management courses through the years we have asked the participants if they consider themselves to be above-average communicators. Almost all declare that they are. We then ask if a sizable amount of their compensation is due to their communicative success. The answers are yes and cover what, to the authors, is an amazing range. The range is that the executives believe that anywhere from 20 percent to 85 percent of their pay is due to their excellence as communicators. Rightly or wrongly, many executives believe that a person who isn't communicating clearly isn't thinking clearly.

22. Why is it that my people often don't do what I told them to do?

A. Because they didn't really understand what you said. For the young manager it is doubtful if there is anything better than the habit of saying to the people with whom he deals, "I would appreciate it if you would tell me right now what your understanding is as to what we have just agreed to." Another method is illustrated by the new executive head of a major bank who found that some of the loans were in bad shape. He started having meetings at night with the responsible officers. After a discussion, the loan officer would agree that he would take specific action. The new president the following day wrote a memo to the loan officer saying, "As I recall our discussion of last evening, you have agreed to do the following things . . . ." He then itemized the first step to "either have the loans repaid in full or some other conclusion satisfactory to you and me arrived at by such-and-such date." All of this is by way of saying that success in managing is made more likely when the following is true:

1. The manager has a clear idea of what he wants to communicate.

2. He does communicate clearly.
3. He then asks the people with whom he has talked to play back to him their understanding of what has been covered.

The young manager's relations with other company employees

23. Should the young manager, as he learns of office politics, take sides or remain neutral? Can he remain neutral and succeed? Are all politics bad and to be avoided?

A. Politics exist in business, in life, everywhere. What some people see as politics is often only the overt or covert attempts by people to influence others to support certain programs or actions. These programs or actions would not necessarily be bad for the company. Sometimes, however, politics appear to be an attempt to subvert the authority or instructions of an upper manager. Politics exist at all levels in most companies. We know that some compromise is frequently necessary between people with opposing views. It is essential that one knows what the compromises are and can give in on factors which might have equal chances for success in a company. However, the authors believe the young manager should never compromise his own principles!

The young manager should gain and retain the respect and confidence of his co-workers, which means that he must usually listen to them, but he must be extremely careful in not taking sides or even appearing to take sides on matters that are not of his immediate concern but come under the general umbrella of "office politics." Not only can he succeed by being neutral, he must be extremely adroit at being neutral so as not to hurt his own chances. By this we mean that if neutrality suggests to his associates that he is lacking in thought, character, and courage, this will hurt him. On the other hand, if he can successfully avoid taking sides in political struggles and do this without appearing prissy or superior, he will end up with both sides respecting him.

24. Should the young manager listen to, or even encourage, the flow of information to him via the grapevine?

A. The rumor mill or grapevine exists in all companies. You can be on it or not as you will. The kinds of stories transmitted are often a measurement of morale. A young manager cannot afford to be ignorant of what is on the grapevine. He cannot necessarily take the information at face value, but neither can he dismiss rumors out of hand as having no significance. So he should listen but be careful about believing what he hears.

25. Is it a good principle or a bad principle for a young manager to give business advice to employees reporting to another manager?

A. First of all, if a young manager does not strike up acquaintanceships with people in other components, he will deprive himself of a great deal of potentially valuable input about the company. On the question of advice, it depends on whether he is asked for it or not. If he is, he should be constructive, ask a lot of questions, try to get the full story, and then on the basis of the facts he has obtained—with common sense, company welfare, and his own career's welfare in mind—help others with genuinely sincere advice. The danger, however, is not getting enough of the facts to be reasonably sure that he understands the problem. For example, employees who are in trouble with their own boss often tend to give a slanted story to another manager and it is dangerous to just accept one side of a story.

26. If a young manager hears of a bad situation in another component from one of its employees, should he tell the manager of that component what he has heard or should he take it to their mutual manager, or should he ignore it?

A. A manager should do whatever he can to help his company. In this case, however, he must be very careful how he tells the other manager, for he can get his informant in trouble on the basis of carrying tales out of school. If he is sufficiently adroit, he can get a reputation for being a constructive co-worker rather than a meddler. Under no circumstances should he ever tell the mutual manager the answer to the apparent problem. Leave that to the person with the problem. A good method to follow is to say in effect to the concerned manager: "You'll have to decide if my story is accurate. An employee of yours volunteered, in confidence, the story I am now going to tell you. (Tells the story.) If the situation were reversed I'd

want you to tell me. I hope you feel what I am doing is OK
and in your interest and the company's."

The young manager's attitude
toward company problems

27. To what extent and under what conditions should the
young manager defend top management's policies?

A. If he knows enough about the rationale for company
policies he should defend them; if he doesn't, he should excuse
himself from commenting until he does. He should never assume
they are poor or bad until he gets the facts—if necessary from
his own manager. One of the hardest lessons for a young manager to learn is that conclusions are not always obvious. There
are usually more facts at higher levels unknown to the lower
levels. Some consideration should be given to this. On the other
hand, a blanket defense of everything without information
merely stamps one as an unthinking yes-man and can do his
career more harm than good.

28. If the young manager hears bad things about his company, should he respond? If so, how?

A. He should respond by asking for all the information he
feels is necessary before venturing an opinion. Neither defense
nor agreement is wise without sufficient facts. As a general
policy, giving the company the benefit of the doubt if any
exists, is wise, and beneficial to the young manager. In fact,
some executives believe if you can't be in agreement most of
the time with company policy, decisions and actions, you should
leave the company.

29. In times of hectic production or engineering requirements,
is it necessary to take the time to keep a good record of actions?

A. The bigger the organization, the more important it is to
keep good records. Even if a 20-hour day is required, take
another half hour to record what was tried and the results
obtained. When emergencies are over, top management often
quickly forgets the urgency of the past situation and the young
manager may easily be criticized for taking unilateral action in
not following standard operating procedure, or whatever. Good
records protect you.

The young manager's optional behavior

30. When a problem situation is being discussed in a meeting, should the young manager put forth his views freely?

A. He should not be the first to put forth his views, because without exception others, often senior to him, have more facts or experiences which may relate to the same problem. It is essential, however, that he speak at some point, or he cannot make any impression. His remarks can be a thoughtful summation of the various views expressed. He should not take a position until he is confident he understands the issues and their probable implications.

31. Should a young manager meet company standards of dress and conduct that are not what he would establish?

A. The old saying, "When in Rome do as the Romans do," is still common sense. An old bromide is, "We're going to run the company our way until such time as you get to be president, and then we'll run it your way."

32. How hard should the young manager work—regular hours only or come in early, stay late, and take work home?

A. Hard enough to get the job done well and a little extra besides. If work is necessary every evening, something is wrong and he had better analyze the situation. If no extra work is ever required, something is also wrong. The old saying, "No man ever got ahead by *not* doing what he was told to do or doing *only* what he was told to do," is still true. The authors believe every man should live a balanced life to achieve happiness as well as business success. To work day and night to the neglect of one's family is wrong. It cannot be made up for later—for the children will be grown and a family break-up may have occurred.

33. To what extent should the young manager walk through other parts of the office or factory? Will he be accused of loitering or going where he isn't wanted?

A. Many young people fail to take advantage of the opportunity of walking through other parts of their company on the way to and from work or even at lunch time. A great deal can be learned, whether it's a financial institution or a factory, by seeing how other components operate. If a man's interest is seen to include more than his immediate area or component, it is a plus. If he stops to ask questions, however, they should be reasonably intelligent ones. If he asks stupid questions, he runs the risk of gaining a reputation for being stupid.

34. Should the young manager ever say, "I don't know"?

A. Of course he should say "I don't know" if something comes up and he doesn't. On the other hand, if it's something he should know the answer to, he should follow it up at once with the statement, "But I'll find out immediately what the answer is and let you know." If the question involves something he should have known, he had better do his homework continuously so he doesn't have to admit ignorance often. Some managers feel they lose face by admitting ignorance. They can lose face faster by pretending knowledge when it's not there, as the follow-up questions will usually prove. A manager we know will ask a question, and if the respondent begins to stall, will break in with, "The answer is yes, no, or I don't know—now which is it?" This approach is of value only when the question is answerable in such straightforward terms; but often the first question is merely preliminary to a second and third of greater depth, and both time and credibility are lost if the young manager does not answer truthfully to the first one.

35. Should the young manager initiate a cost reduction program or spend much effort on improving productivity?

A. A young manager should be alert to the fact that, if unchecked, costs always rise. Too often cost reduction programs or improved productivity programs are suggested or imposed by the top management. The young manager has a continuous opportunity and should be alert to this universal need to reduce costs, and should initiate such action.

36. Should a young manager fight for his principles?

A. Yes. We believe it is axiomatic that if a man is not honest, his co-workers and employees will find it out. Similarly, if he cheats or steals, he will not succeed nor should he. Over and beyond these elementary principles, a young manager should hold to principles of fair play, equal treatment to all employees, and honesty with vendors and customers. As difficult issues arise—as profit pressure grows—as desire to advancement increases, a young manager may believe he can gain an advantage by cutting corners, by "giving up" on a principle. An example is a decision to improve profits by withholding from outstanding workers their just due, or by paying people less than they should be paid even though this is against his principle of treating people equitably. The authors believe a man should carry the fight himself or, if the boss is the source of the suggestion, fight his boss rather than give up on principle. We believe over the long run a man's career is advanced by standing on principle.

37. Can a young manager keep his integrity and also succeed in business?

A. Not only can he keep his integrity and succeed, but the odds are that he *must* keep his integrity to succeed. We know some rascals succeed in business. However, it is the authors' observation that most of the rewards in business go to men of integrity.

38. Can the young manager ever afford to lose his temper completely and blow up?

A. Once in a while, yes. Every man or woman is entitled to go to this point, but not very often. And if injudicious things are said or actions taken, they must be corrected immediately when normal temper is regained. One manager of rather short temper whom we know budgets his blow-ups to not more than one every six months.

39. Do I need a high level of energy in order to be a very successful manager?

A. Generally, yes—just as most sports require a high level. One necessary attribute of good management is leadership, and people find it difficult to find leadership in a person who is lethargic, sleepy-appearing, or even apathetic.

40. Can a young manager really succeed as a manager without having a lot of self-confidence?

A. No—not really. People are not inclined to commit themselves to a course of action and fight hard to make them succeed if their manager appears unsure of that course. We think Corinthians I 14:8 is right on the beam when it says, "For if the trumpet give an uncertain sound, who shall prepare himself for the battle?"

41. Does a young manager have enough time to do all the things his manager expects him to do?

A. Generally, yes he does. He often forgets that his manager came through these jobs himself and knows what it takes to do them properly. If the young manager finds he is hopelessly snowed under with too much work, he should discuss the situation with his manager. Often he is spending too much time on minor matters, or at least a lot more than the manager expects.

42. In my budget, should I have an undisclosed kitty of time and money?

A. No, you'll be found out sooner or later. It's likely to be sooner if you and your people only work at three-quarter speed or only commit three quarters of the available resources. It is better to make best-effort estimates and fight to make them. A kitty known to your boss—and approved by him—is a different matter.

43. If a young manager is not going to make his plan, how should he deal with his boss?

A. It is imperative that he tell the boss *before* the due date. If there are situations/conditions beyond his control he should specify them. Under no circumstances should he blame others for his failures. An alibi is never well accepted—a good reason, something completely beyond the young manager's control, is acceptable but it must be offered *before* the job is supposed to be finished.

44. Does it really pay the young manager to write down what problems he is facing and to spell them out in detail?

A. Yes, just as many problems tend to be clarified by discussion with another, so writing them down often helps make them clear. Also, possible solutions can be written and considered. In addition, the chosen solution written down can be carefully studied before a decision is made. These are good techniques.

45. How can a young manager gain visibility and a good press with top management of his company?

A. There are many ways. By always doing more than is asked for and doing it well; by getting and implementing creative ideas; by getting fans who extol his good points; by treating all people well so they in turn speak well of him; by doing good things in the community which reflect credit on the company.

These are a few ways and if a young manager decides to build a career plan, he should make such things part of his strategy. (Career planning is discussed in Chapter 12.)

46. To what extent should a spouse be told about work? Nothing? Everything?

A. Depends on the spouse. If problems are involved, it is usually best to leave the spouse ignorant of the facts, especially if they are natural worriers. If the spouse can be a constructive element, then it may well be good to discuss matters, but the failing or shortcomings of co-workers should *never* be brought home.

47. Should the young manager continue to take courses at night school after he gets a job?

A. Many young managers overdo this. If the course will help directly and specifically with the job, perhaps so, but another degree won at night school is not as valuable to success as the same amount of study directed to job-related situations.

48. Should the young manager read the same newspapers and trade magazines that his manager does?

A. Yes.

49. When the young manager sees a better job opening in his company, even though he may not be fully qualified to fill it, should he ask for it?

A. Yes, if he wants it. He may not get it, but he probably establishes himself in his boss's mind as an ambitious comer.

50. What are some things a manager just promoted into a new job should do?

A. Here are some things a young man can/should do in the first two months on the job. In the area of your assignment:

1. Learn who else besides your boss is important in the operation.
2. Find out who gives orders to your boss; he may come by and talk to you. Many have been most surprised by not recognizing a name and then later finding out that they were talking to their boss's boss. Then the soul-searching starts to remember what was said by both parties, so you can tell your boss the highlights of the discussion.

3. Get an organizational chart. Find out if it is real or imaginary.
4. Study the information flow of your component and the material flow.
5. Start to learn ratios by asking questions such as: What do you consider a good measurement? What about sales per employee? What about output per square foot? What about productivity? Sales per dollar of investment?
6. Ask the knowledgeable people around you what they consider are the major problems in the component, if any. This may precipitate violent, anti-personnel comments such as, "The boss is our major problem." If so, don't "buy" that idea. Make up your own mind.
7. Learn what trade magazines your boss reads and immediately subscribe to them and read them carefully.
8. Find out what is expected of you and whether that is what you will be measured on. Get a copy of the appraisal form if at all possible. Is the appraisal done by your boss only or is there more than one rater?

51. Does a manager only direct the work of others?

A. Not if he is smart. He should also make a personal contribution. A highly successful general manager asks his managers: "What personal contribution have you made to the success of your business? What, but for you, would not have happened?" He goes on to say, "I am not asking you to ask yourself if last year and this year you have been loyal, hard-working, and a good team player. Nor am I asking such questions as did you follow company policy, did you follow standard operating procedures, did you answer the phone and mail promptly and attend all meetings you were asked to? I am instead asking you to tell me what contribution did you alone—as an individual—make to your division last year—and the year to date? What is the thing which but for you would not have been explored—would not have been started—would not have been accomplished?"

Our manager friend gave an example. He said that a leading retailer for many years in their delivery service had a truck driver and helper. The operating manager to whom the delivery manager reported asked, "Why should they have a helper?" *Answer:* "Someone has to be in the truck so that the goods left in the truck will not be stolen while the other man takes the package to the door."

The operating manager asked: "Why don't we put a padlock on the door of the truck?" *Answer:* "It takes two men to carry furniture."

The operating manager said, "I am not talking about furniture trucks—I'm talking about parcel trucks."

The upshot of the whole thing was that it was deemed feasible to eliminate the helper without hurting the customers or the service and at a significant savings to the company. This was an individual contribution which but for the operating manager would not have been made.

An interesting question for any manager to ask himself is, "What should be the dollar value of an individual contribution which you make every year?" Someone has said if a man's income is $20,000 a year, he should make a personal individual contribution to the business that would add $200,000 to the pre-tax profits. What do you think?

The young manager's knowledge of business

52. Should the young manager really understand the book-keeping and accounting system and the essentials of financial management and control?

A. He should, and well, and fast. It is the management language of the business. If he needs help, he should ask someone, perhaps a friend of his in the controller's office, to explain it all to him. There are also excellent books available in accounting, financial planning, and control.

53. How much does a young manager have to know about the business itself in order to be successful, or is knowledge of management principles and people enough?

A. The more you know about the business you are in, the better are your chances of success. Many theorists believe that you don't have to know the business. We disagree. If you don't, how can you deal with company problems as well as appraise proposed actions and actual results?

54. Are the management systems the same for all industries?

A. Heavens, no! Each industry has its own most significant measurements and it behooves every young manager to quickly learn what they are. In the department store field, for example, some of the measurements include sales per square foot, sales per employee, selling costs as a percent of net sales, operating costs percent to net sales, profit percent to sales, profits to assets employed, and profit to equity.

55. Many corporations say people are their greatest asset and yet young managers get judged by their figure results instead of by how much they and their people have grown and developed? Why?

A. American business keeps books primarily for Uncle Sam. That is to say that a great deal of corporate accounting is really the basis for making out a tax return and only incidentally to help managers manage. It is true that monthly income or profit and loss statements (P&Ls) are produced, but they usually appear some days after the conclusion of the month and really tell a story of where the corporation has been but are of only nominal value in the current management of the business. Nevertheless, business is strongly oriented toward the figures produced by P&L statements and balance sheets. In addition, various segments of the business have special reports dealing with such things as sales and production.

The managers to whom young managers report are thoroughly oriented to figures. They may not be figure specialists themselves, but figures really represent an important aspect of their corporate life and managing. In fact, an important part of the evaluation of many managers is based on figures. However, another key matter is knowledge of people and what makes them tick and the ability to deal with them effectively.

Starting out in the industrial revolution and going through the era of child labor in this country and into the 1930s, labor was regarded a good deal of the time as being a commodity. Just as you bought coke and ore to make steel, you also bought labor to make the steel. In recent years, and particularly since the Employment Act of 1946 which directed the federal government to attempt to order its policies so that full employment would result, managers have quit thinking of labor as a commodity. Managers have become increasingly concerned with unions, and also with the workers as individuals. Since the Hawthorne Study and other social and behavioralistic studies, as well as the development of theories as to what motivates people, the whole idea of the importance of the individual has grown. All this and more has been summarized by many companies by saying, "People are our greatest asset."

Increasingly, young managers need to become experts in understanding their employees—helping them not only in producing satisfactory to superior results, but also in their personal growth and development. This is a requirement for success in the future. It is rewarding in many ways to the young manager and tends to improve the quality of life, in business, of his people.

56. Must a young manager train and develop a successor?

A. It all depends on the company he works for. In some businesses a manager can't be promoted unless he has a good replacement developed. Find out if this is true in your business. If your company does not have such a requirement, figure out if you want your people to grow and develop. Figure out if you'll help them grow. If you do, you're likely to develop a successor. Level with yourself, would that be an accomplishment or a threat to your security? If you are good and ambitious, and grow yourself, you ought to be ready for promotion by the time your replacement is qualified to fill your position. If you get promoted—great. If not, what to do depends on your personal career plan. (Career planning is discussed in Chapter 12.)

Index

221